What people are saying

The "good news" of the Gospe. never hear it. We want our families, friends, and coworkers to know the Gospel, but we often feel inadequate and unprepared to start a spiritual conversation. No more! Here is an uncomplicated book that gives practical, step-by-step ways to share the Gospel effectively. We can do this! Preston and Kelly explain the full, biblical foundation for each concept, while giving us the confidence to begin "speaking the truth in love" right now.

—James K. Walker, President
Watchman Fellowship, Inc.

"Preston ties the word of God into evangelism in an excellent manner. His high view of Scripture is seen throughout this book. One can clearly see in these pages he is extending the call for Christians to come back to the scriptures. This is vital for evangelism and discipleship to flourish."

—Dr. Mike Napier, Personal Evangelism Specialist
Baptist General Convention of Oklahoma

"What a great tool Preston and Kelly have created. They have definitely done their homework. It is filled with scripture resources and will answer many questions that people have in regard to sharing their faith."

—Mickey Rapier, Lead Pastor
Fellowship Bible Church of Northwest Arkansas

"Preston and Kelly Condra have done the church a favor. *By Which We Are Saved* is a concise theological apologetic that is highly accessible to the average layman. A quick read of this handbook will prepare you for sharing Christ with your neighbor, coworker, or lost family. And more importantly it will serve as a resource to answer their best faith questions about what we as Christians believe. I encourage you to read it, use it, and come back to it often."

—Dr. Jeff Crawford
President, Cross Church School of Ministry

by which we are saved

SHARING THE GOSPEL WITH CONFIDENCE

Preston Condra

Kelly Condra

By Which We Are Saved
Sharing the Gospel with Confidence
Preston Condra and Kelly Condra
Sufficient Word Publishing
Revised

Published by Sufficient Word Publishing, Springdale, AR
Copyright ©2016 Preston Condra and Kelly Condra
All rights reserved.

Back cover photography: Linda Richards, lindarichardsphotography.com

Cover and Interior design: Davis Creative, DavisCreative.com

Library of Congress Cataloging-in-Publication Data
Library of Congress Control Number: 2016957835
Preston Condra and Kelly Condra
By Which We Are Saved: Sharing the Gospel with Confidence
ISBN: 9781946245007
Library of Congress subject headings:
1. REL030000 Evangelism   2. REL067030 Apologetics
3. REL006700 Bible Study

2016

This book is dedicated to
the Body of Christ
that it may have every advantage
in helping others to know
the Gospel that saves.

We are thankful to those who
took the time to read the manuscript,
write endorsements, give feedback,
encourage, and pray.

Table of Contents

*Please review the Index of Objections. It is your guide to making this book useful as a resource handbook.

FOR THE WORK OF THE MINISTRY

For the perfecting of the saints, for the work of the ministry,
for the edifying of the body of Christ. (Eph 4:12)

Our relationship began with lively conversations about politics and religion, and these subjects remain our favorites. We love America and the Constitution and the Bible, and we never tire of talking about them. We are thankful that God has used our unique system of government and its protection of freedom to facilitate prosperity and enable the worldwide proclamation of the Gospel of Christ. Efforts to marginalize the church and dismantle the nation which helped it flourish are disconcerting, and speaking with others about our concerns can be difficult. We believe it is no coincidence that Satan, the Ruler of this Age and the promoter of "political correctness," discourages the discussion of our earthly freedoms and our heavenly position, both of which hamper his agenda.

It is hard to believe that our society has changed so much that sharing the love of Christ might be characterized as "hate," and that preaching from the scripture could be considered a crime. Everywhere we look, Anti-Christ philosophies seem more prominent than Christian values, and some to whom we witness will attend church on Sunday, and fight for pro-choice rights on Monday. Sometimes we just look at each other and say, "How can these things be happening?"

The marginalization of the church has led to a culture shift of a magnitude almost unimaginable just a few decades ago. With the shift, our assumptions have changed in regard to evangelism. For example, we rarely ask anyone if they are "Christian," because it does not mean what it used to. As America changes, so do many churches; we cannot assume that those who attend church will share our worldview. They may not hear a clear Gospel on Sunday morning or even believe that the Bible is true. Among those who are not church-affiliated, the gap is even wider: the normalization of things such as drug legalization and gender reassignment are not even shocking to them.

As Christianity continues to lose prominence in society, believers fear for their friendships, their livelihoods, and even their freedom for standing on Biblical principles. Not wanting to offend, attract the label of "religious fanatic," or be the next victim of world-wide media attention, many avoid religious discussion altogether. Others are willing, but tell us they are not equipped to handle the questions and objections which may arise in a conversation about their faith. As Christian beliefs and practices have been systematically eliminated from our society, we feel strongly that we must further the ongoing work of the church to encourage and prepare believers for evangelism and to integrate it more fully into everyday life.

If our nation's altered worldview, society's hostility, and the risk of personal attack are not barriers enough, those who oppose the Gospel are not the only obstacle to successful evangelism. Some segments of Christendom promote "simplified" versions of the Gospel, altered with well-intentions, but lacking in clarity and accuracy.

So, the believer's dilemma is that while the culture increasingly opposes Christianity, our call to proclaim the Gospel remains, and the world's need for it grows. Although we will face resistance to the Gospel, it is possible to discuss it without being found offensive. There are still people who have questions and want to talk about faith, the Bible and eternity. They may not dare to start a "politically incorrect" conversation themselves, but they will be glad that someone else is willing.

It is because witnessing can be daunting, discouraging, and difficult in many ways that we wish to make a contribution toward the best possible outcome, utilizing both biblical truth and human advice. The mere existence of the many objections to the Gospel reveals the necessity of an accurate and thorough explanation of who Jesus is, what He did for us, why we need it, and how we receive it. The first chapter of this book is a detailed explanation of the Gospel and some of its supporting doctrines. Because the politically correct culture demands care in how we evangelize, Chapter two contains suggestions for self-examination and communication to help a Christian witness prepare himself for initiating and furthering biblical conversations. The balance of the book contains objections to the Gospel and the Bible's response. Its focus on scripture enables witnesses to offer God's answers, thus preventing a contest of opinions. Although this is a resource handbook, we believe Chapters one and two will benefit every reader; the others can be used as needed. The Gospel's elements overlap; verses in one section may help with other objections. Please review the Index of Objections; it is your guide to making the book useful.

We have three hopes for this book. The first is to promote a thorough explanation of the Gospel in witnessing situations. The second is

3

that this resource will engender confidence about engaging others in biblically-related conversations. Our third hope for this book is that it will be marked up and dog-eared because it is often used to answer the questions of hearers.

The Gospel can be simply believed with the faith of a child, but it can also be misunderstood in many ways. Our emphasis, therefore, is trusting the testimony of God's word, knowing that one cannot be argued into heaven. As Christian evangelists, we do our part by initiating conversations about Biblical topics, explaining the Gospel, offering scriptural answers to questions and praying for the hearer. We know the Holy Spirit works to draw mankind through the preaching of the Gospel, as He convicts every sinner of his need. By providing a thoroughly-explained Gospel message and a biblical response to objections, we fulfill our calling as Christians to function as ministers of the Gospel of Christ and facilitate the Spirit's work.

Satan wants us to believe that we are not equipped to share the Gospel, or that it is too risky to do so, but, on the contrary, we are to be a light to a dying world! As the body of Christ, we are to build up one another in the work of the ministry. We pray that this book will be found helpful in sharing the Gospel of Christ effectively with a world that desperately needs its good news.

Preston and Kelly

> *Moreover, brethren, I declare unto you the gospel which I preached unto you, which also ye have received, and wherein ye stand; By which also ye are saved...* (1 Cor 15:1-2)

CHAPTER 1

THE GOSPEL BY WHICH WE ARE SAVED

The Gospel of Christ

*1 Moreover, brethren, I declare unto you the gospel which I preached unto you, which also ye have received, and wherein ye stand; 2 **By which also ye are saved,** if ye keep in memory what I preached unto you, unless ye have believed in vain. 3 For I delivered unto you first of all that which I also received, how that Christ died for our sins according to the scriptures; 4 And that he was buried, and that he rose again the third day according to the scriptures: 5 And that he was seen of Cephas, then of the twelve: 6 After that, he was seen of above five hundred brethren at once; of whom the greater part remain unto this present, but some are fallen asleep. 7 After that, he was seen of James; then of all the apostles. 8 And last of all he was seen of me also, as of one born out of due time.*
(1Cor 15:1-8, emphasis added)

The Main Event

The "good news," or Gospel message, is contained in 1 Corinthians 15:1-8, which declares it to be the message *by which* we are saved. In Romans 1:16, this message is given a title by Paul, who calls it the "Gospel of Christ," the power of God unto salvation. Although other verses such as John 3:16 and Ephesians 2:8-9 contain additional information about salvation, 1 Corinthians 15: 3-4 is the essential core of the Gospel, namely the death, burial, and resurrection of Jesus Christ for our sins, and therefore contains the object of faith for salvation.

For the purposes of this book, we refer to the Gospel as 1 Corinthians 15:1-4, because we believe that verses 1-2 are worthy of inclusion in a Gospel presentation. They identify the passage as the saving Gospel message, and provide a warning about believing in vain, a factual belief without the intended purpose of salvation. We sometimes include verses 5-8 which declare proof of the resurrection verified by hundreds of witnesses.

Because Satan can twist every aspect of the Gospel, knowing and understanding its elements is essential for recognizing and answering misdirected belief, misunderstandings, and various erroneous ideas about salvation. Many unsaved people are assumed to be Christian until a conversation arises in which beliefs that contradict the Gospel come to light. We have met sincere people who initially seem to agree that Jesus died for their sins, but upon further discussion, they reveal definitions of Jesus, salvation, or other Gospel elements which differ from the Biblical meaning of these terms. Because each part of the Gospel is necessary, misunderstanding or denying part of the Gospel is equivalent to not believing the Gospel at all. Therefore, we exhort believers to know the Gospel well and to use 1 Corinthians 15:1-4 when witnessing.

Although the Gospel contains necessary elements, it is not simply a formula. Each hearer of the Gospel may have his own ideas about God, eternity, and religion, as well as many questions. Regardless of the objections raised or questions asked in a witnessing situation, a Christian who thoroughly knows the Gospel can connect the conversation back to the Gospel element to which the question relates. Doing so keeps the conversation Bible-centered, making God the authority, not the Christian witness. We wish not only to help Christians offer a clear and accurate Gospel, but to avoid making the conversation a battle of wills or a debate.

The five elements of the Gospel of Christ are labeled in this book as who, what, why, how and where. Briefly, they are as follows:

Who: Jesus Christ, God the Son, the one and only Savior of sinners, and the one and only way of salvation.

What: The death, burial and resurrection of Jesus Christ on the cross for sins, as a substitute for the sins of mankind, taking upon Himself the wrath of God against sin.

Why: Jesus died for us because every human being is a sinner and under penalty of death for sinning against God. As finite human beings we cannot "make up for" or "undo" our sins and are therefore facing eternal suffering in the lake of fire, the permanent residence of those who will pay for their own sins.

How: We can be saved from the penalty of sin by grace through faith. God graciously grants deliverance to each who believes the Gospel of Christ, 1 Corinthians 15:3-4, and who does so for the purpose of his own salvation, apart from works of any kind.

Where: Twice in the Gospel we find the phrase, "according to the scriptures," a reference to the source of the saving message. Because the Bible is the revelation of Jesus Christ and the source of the Gospel, disbelief in the Bible can be a barrier to accepting the truth of its message.

The Backstory

In addition to the essential elements of the Gospel of Christ, there are several Biblical teachings which underpin the Gospel, and are helpful for believers to understand in order to explain some objections to it. These teachings include the meaning of spiritual birth, the substitutionary sacrifice of Jesus, man's position in the family of Adam, the placement of the believer into the body of Christ, the necessity of the faith system for salvation, and the Bible as God's written revelation of Himself.

There is great benefit in understanding the Gospel thoroughly, but no benefit in assuming that those with whom we share the Gospel already possess accurate definitions of its elements. Of all the potential objections to the Gospel, the most common is the mainstay of false religion: works for salvation. A broader understanding of the doctrines related to salvation can be used to show that salvation by faith is a spiritual transaction, and is therefore distinct from human efforts of any kind.

Because the Bible is the exclusive source of every Christian doctrine, we find that witnessing goes more smoothly if we begin by asking a hearer about his view of scripture. The balance of this chapter, starting with the case for addressing the Bible as a potential objection, contains explanations of some of the supporting doctrines of the Gospel, as well as the Gospel elements themselves.

The Source of the Gospel is the Bible

Creation itself reveals the existence of a Creator, but the general revelation of God's existence does not reveal His identity, nor how to enter into a relationship with Him. We need more information than the creation around us to know who God is. So, how can we know Him, and know that His message is true? He provided two proofs of Himself: He walked among us in the person of Jesus Christ, and He provided a written record revealing Himself. The Bible is our trustworthy historical record which reveals God the Son and the message of salvation, the Gospel.

The Gospel of Christ, found in 1 Corinthians 15:1-4, contains the phrase "according to the scriptures" twice, suggesting that the trustworthiness of the source of the message is inextricable from the facts of the saving message. For this reason, we encourage Christian witnesses to ask a hearer's opinion of the Bible when sharing the Gospel. Those who have a general respect for the Bible may be willing to consider what it says, while a person who does not trust the Bible may not be ready to believe its saving message or even listen to its testimony. From his perspective, he is being asked to entrust his eternal destiny to a message from an unreliable source.

Unbelief that is rooted in distrust of the Bible creates a dilemma for witnessing and an obstacle for salvation, since it is the Bible itself wherein all proof lies. An article or a book written to offer evidence of the Bible as a supernatural revelation from God and a reliable historical record may be a better place to begin with those who object to the Bible. Learning early if there is hostility or indifference toward the Bible can avoid frustration for both the Christian and the hearer in a witnessing situation. Discussing the trustworthiness of the Bible may help an initially dismissive objector realize that he has no concrete reasons for doubting its testimony. If, on the other hand, he voices strong objections, quoting verses of scripture may not be the best starting point for a discussion of faith and eternity. We would not tell a Christian witness not to quote scripture, as the Holy Spirit uses the words of scripture to teach us the truth of the Gospel (Jn 16:13). We ask only that Christians exercise discernment; a hearer may refuse to consider the word of God, but he may be willing to learn why so many others believe it.

Christian Salvation is a Spiritual Birth

The biblical concept of a spiritual birth is one that we have found is not well understood, even among Christians. It is a unique teaching, one that was difficult for even a learned religious leader of Israel to understand (Jn 3:4). Although it may not be necessary to explain the details of spiritual birth when witnessing, a discussion about the Gospel often reveals what may be the world's most common religious belief, that one must perform rituals or good works to appease or impress "god." An explanation of the Christian spiritual birth is sometimes needed in order to distinguish religious works from spiritual salvation.

Christianity stands alone in teaching that no one has ever been saved by law-keeping, a clean life, or works of any kind. The Bible tells us instead that we must be "born again" (Jn 3:7). But Christians and non-Christians alike may hold views of Christianity which make it seem like a social activity or membership in a civic group. It is important for hearers to know that our faith is not simply a lifestyle of goodness, church attendance and giving. While morality, helpfulness and fellowship are meant to be products of a spiritual birth, there are many decent, philanthropic, community-minded non-Christians. Therefore, such outward traits cannot define Christianity; they are a result of it. It is possible for someone to give verbal assent to the death, burial, and resurrection of Jesus, while still holding on to a belief in works for salvation.

Helpful for comprehending the Christian spiritual birth is knowing more about birth and death according to scripture. For example, the death of a person does not result in his annihilation or non-existence. When a person's physical body stops functioning, that person lives on. Death can be viewed, therefore, as a separation. The material part of man, the body, is in the grave, separated from the immaterial soul and spirit, which continue to live.

The human spirit is the part of man which can be connected to God. God is the only source of spiritual life, which is why we refer to our relationship with him as spiritual. A person can be physically alive and yet be spiritually dead because he is separated from the source of spiritual life (Eph 2:1). To be spiritually born means that one's human spirit is in communion with, meaning connected with, God. Other references to aspects of the born-again spiritual condition include "the new birth," being "born from above," "begotten again," "indwelt," and "regenerated." Awareness of the various terms can aid communication when witnessing.

In addition to knowing that being "born again" refers to our spiritual connection with God, we recommend that Christians know a little of humanity's background in relation to spirituality. A brief history of human spiritual life begins with Adam, who was created sinless and in spiritual communion with God. God told Adam that if he ate from the tree of the knowledge of good and evil, he would die (Gen 3:3).

But Adam did not drop dead upon eating it. Although he *began* dying physically, his immediate death was spiritual. God could no longer commune with Adam's spirit because it was now tainted with sin.

When Adam ate from the tree, he was making a decision to act independently of God's will. His act of disobedience was sin, and, therefore, he became separated from a holy God who cannot commune with sin. Neither could God commune with any of Adam's descendants. Although Adam was created in the likeness of God, the Bible tells us that after he sinned, Adam's children were created in *his* likeness; they were sinners (Gen 5:1-3). Having sinned, Adam no longer possessed the quality of being spiritually alive and, therefore, could not pass on to his descendants that which he no longer had. As a result of being part of Adam's family, we are born separated from God, just as Adam became separated when he rebelled in the garden (Gen 3:6). This is why every person is born a sinner, and why the Bible refers to unsaved humanity as being "in Adam," a doctrine we will cover later in this chapter.

The intimate spiritual connection enjoyed by Adam could not be restored until sin no longer stood between God and man. The restoration of spiritual communion was accomplished when God the Son died for sin on the cross (Ro 5:10; 2 Cor 5:18-19). With all sin having been paid, God can now commune with any man who has accepted that payment for his own sins (1 Cor 15:22).

In summary, all men are born spiritually dead, separated from God by sin, and in need of a Savior. To escape the punishment for sin, we must each be cleansed from sin by accepting Jesus' payment for sin on our behalf. Upon believing the Gospel, we are no longer separated from

God by sin. We are saved from damnation, made part of a spiritual family, able to enjoy a relationship with God, and destined for heaven.

Learning about the need for spiritual birth can be vital to a correct understanding of the Gospel. Those who see the Christian faith as simply a lifestyle choice may have convinced themselves and others that they are Christians, without having been born again. If they claim to be Christian, who would think to share the Gospel with them? But if they have not believed the Gospel, they remain separated from God. We believe that to fulfill the Christian calling to share the Gospel, we must do more than briefly mention the death, burial and resurrection for sins. By asking hearers to tell us what they believe about the elements of the Gospel message, we can address any misunderstandings they have about it which may not be readily apparent.

Jesus is God, the One and Only Savior of Mankind

Understanding the spiritual nature of the Christian faith is often needed to distinguish it from works when sharing the Gospel. But central to the Gospel message is the Savior Himself. Explaining Jesus is not easy. The Gospel verses do not plainly say "Jesus is God." But could someone be saved who denied that Jesus was God? If Jesus is simply a man and not God, could a person's faith in an ordinary man save him, even if that man was an extraordinary example of altruism, forgiveness, and love?

Because some hearers believe that Jesus was only a man, a Christian witness needs to be able to explain a few things about the Savior of mankind. Doing so is foundational to providing further explanation about what He did for us. For example, an ordinary man cannot also be mankind's Savior. He would have no way to pay for the sins of others, because he would have his own to pay for. His death on a cross would not solve the problem of sin between God and man, because it would be followed by the penalty God requires for every man: eternal separation in the lake of fire (Rev 20:15). There must be something unique about the One who took the infinite sins of the world upon Himself. He was not just some great guy who died to set an example of sacrificial love or to make a statement about forgiveness, as some believe.

One way to address the need for the Savior to be God is to relay the enormity of the sin problem, as well as the seriousness of having offended God. Because the sins of mankind are a problem of infinite proportions, paying for those sins requires an infinite payment. Either a sinner will spend an infinity paying for sin (Rev 20:10-14), or his sins must be laid upon an infinite person. In other words, the Savior of the world would have to be our infinite God. Additionally, in order to be a substitute for mankind, and specifically a replacement for Adam as the head of the human family, the Savior would have to be a man. Jesus is the only one who fulfills both requirements: He is fully God, who took on a human nature and body to become fully man also (Phil 2:6, Col 2:9, Heb 2:6). In so doing, He was a just and infinite substitute for man, and a sacrifice for the sins of mankind, making Himself the recipient of God's wrath against sin.

Jesus is God in the flesh, and contrary to the prevalent belief that Jesus is one of many equally valid ways of salvation, He is the one and only Savior of mankind. The Gospel is not compatible with, "You have your way; I have mine." Because of Jesus' exclusive claims, one cannot believe that there are other "saviors" or other ways to be saved while at the same time believing the Gospel (Acts 4:12, Jn 8:12, 10:9, 14:6).

A person who considers Jesus to be one religious prophet, messenger, or savior among many does not believe in the true Jesus Christ, but a false Christ of his own creation. Therefore, the object of that man's faith is vain, meaning it is of no use for the purpose of saving. The object of saving faith must be the correct object, namely, Jesus Christ, God the Son, the Savior of the world (1 Cor 15:2, 2 Cor 11:4). When sharing the Gospel, asking a hearer to explain what he understands about Jesus is of great importance for him to understand in what and in whom he is being asked to place his faith for salvation.

Jesus Paid for Our Sins by Dying on a Cross

Jesus is at the center of the Gospel message. To be saved, one must believe in what He did: that He died for sins on a cross, was buried and rose again, according to the scriptures. Some hearers may question what Jesus did and why He did it. For example, many people died on crosses; what was different about this death? Why was a cross the method of Jesus' death and what did it achieve?

Jesus had to die because the shedding of blood is the method that Almighty God chose for paying a debt to Him. Leviticus 17:11 informs us that life is in the blood, and we know that losing one's blood is certain death. Hebrews 9:22 teaches that without the shedding of blood is no remission, referring to the remission of sins. We see blood sacrifice after the fall in Genesis 4:3-5 and in the Law of Moses. When God the Son came to earth to be a sacrifice for all mankind, He took on a human body and shed His blood, giving His life for ours.

Jesus' death was unique because it fulfilled prophecy, allowing Jesus to be identified by Israel as its Messiah. The Bible does not explain why

God chose crucifixion as the manner of death, but this horrific method does seem to highlight the seriousness of sin. Under the Law of Moses, dying on a tree signified being cursed by God, pointing to the destiny of all sinners (Deut 21:22-23, Gal 3:13, Jn 3:18).

Looking again to the first man, Adam, we can see what Jesus' death actually achieved. In 1 Corinthians 15:45, Jesus is called the "last Adam." 1 Corinthians 15:22 states, "For as in Adam all die, even so in Christ shall all be made alive." Jesus became Adam's substitute as head of the human race; when God the Father poured out His wrath against sin onto Jesus Christ, making Him sin for us, He was moving the accountability for sin to Jesus (2 Cor 5:21). Because Jesus' sacrifice for sin paid the debt originally incurred by Adam and took the punishment we deserved for our sins, a spiritual connection with God was once again made possible. All who accept Jesus' payment for their sins are reconciled to God.

Because every human being is a descendant of Adam, we are all reckoned by God to be sinners "in Adam," and disqualified from having a relationship with God. Being "in Adam" means to be under the headship of Adam, the head of the human race, and part of Adam's family. Each person who places his faith in the Gospel of Christ is immediately credited with Christ's righteousness. God counts every believer to be righteous "in Christ," and transfers him from the human family of Adam to the spiritual family of God. This transaction happens in the mind of God; it is not something we can see. Our new spiritual location is known as the Christian's position "in Christ," and the placing of us there is known as Holy Spirit baptism. The new spiritual entity created by this spiritual transaction is called "the body of Christ" and has Christ as its head instead of Adam (Ro 6:3; 1 Cor12:13). Holy Spirit baptism is one of two spiritual transactions which occur when a person believes the Gospel. The other is regeneration, also known as being "born again," as explained earlier in this chapter.

Jesus died on a cross for our sins because we are sinners who need a savior from God's wrath against sin. Jesus' death saves us because He paid both a physical and a spiritual price for sin, just as Adam did. He was a physical human substitute for mankind, replacing the first man, Adam, as the representative of the human race, and dying in our place for sin. He was also the object of God's wrath in the spiritual punishment for our sins, having been "made sin for us" (2 Cor 5:21). Having been declared guilty of the sins of the world, He was spiritually forsaken, separated from fellowship with the Father and the Holy Spirit while He hung on the cross (Mt 27:46b, Mk 15:31). Having a deeper understanding of the purpose and significance of Jesus' death can make it easier to explain to others exactly what Jesus did and why we need it.

We Access the Gospel by Faith

Every person is a sinner who is in need of a savior from sin. Jesus Christ, God the Son, is that Savior, revealed in God's word, the Bible. We access salvation by believing the Gospel of Christ, found in 1 Corinthians 15:1-4.

Believing the Gospel is also known as having faith in it. To have faith means to be persuaded that something is true and, therefore, to trust in it (Ro 4:21; Heb 11:13). In describing the believer's relationship to God, Paul tells us, "It is by faith that it might be by grace" (Ro 4:16). The word "grace" can be translated as "undeserved favor," and receiving a favor is the opposite of working to earn something. Because we cannot both receive a gift and work to earn it, grace is contrasted with work. As an illustration, when I work, my employer is indebted to me, meaning I am owed wages for that work (Ro 4:4). The wages I earn are not a gift. However, when something is a gift of grace, it was not earned and not even deserved; it was just given.

It is important to note that there is no merit that I can claim for myself in recognizing what someone else has accomplished. Therefore, when I believe in what Christ did, I am not indebting God to me, as I would if I had earned what I received. My faith in the death, burial, and resurrection of Jesus Christ upon the cross for sin is a belief, and has nothing whatsoever to do with my acumen, abilities or achievements. In faith, I am looking away from myself to the work of another; I am trusting Him, and in what He did for me. Therefore, what I receive in return for my faith is gracious: I owe nothing for it. Because God loved me in Christ, in that spiritual transaction on the cross, He can freely give me the gift of salvation when I place my faith in the Gospel message (Ro 5:15-18, 6:23; Eph 2:8-9, Titus 3:5a). I am accepting what He did out of His love, and mercy, and goodness.

Any belief in works must be eliminated in order to accept the Gospel of Christ by faith. Just as it did in the garden, even one sin would separate me from God and disqualify me from earning salvation by good works. It is only by the faith system that God can provide salvation, so that it can be given as a free gift, by grace. It must be so, as no man could ever earn it.

Acts 13: A Real-Life Example of Witnessing

Although the Gospel contains necessary elements, because of the wide variations of belief among hearers, it cannot be used as a simple formula. A thorough understanding of its context and underlying truths enables Christians to answer questions and objections with confidence and clarity, explaining the "who, what, why, and how" of the Gospel, and defending the "where" if needed. When Paul shared the Gospel, it is unlikely that he simply recited the Gospel without offering any explanation. The most thorough record of Paul presenting the Gospel is found in Acts 13, where he is speaking to a group of Jews. If he had been speaking to Gentiles who didn't know the Old Testament scriptures, he may not have explained it exactly in this way; he might have excluded Israel's history, for example. We can safely assume, however, that the elements of the Gospel by which we are saved would have been included, as well as answers to the questions of his audience. Because this passage from Acts 13 includes both the basics of the Gospel and many supporting truths behind those elements, it is worthy of careful study. Here we provide some context, followed by a comparison, using a brief description of the elements he mentions alongside the corresponding verse:

15 And after the reading of the law and the prophets the rulers of the synagogue sent unto them, saying, Ye men and brethren, if ye have any word of exhortation for the people, say on. 16 Then Paul stood up, and beckoning with his hand said, Men of Israel, and ye that fear God, give audience. 17 The God of this people of Israel chose our fathers, and exalted the people when they dwelt

as strangers in the land of Egypt, and with an high arm brought
he them out of it. 18 And about the time of forty years suffered he
their manners in the wilderness. 19 And when he had destroyed
seven nations in the land of Canaan, he divided their land to
them by lot. 20 And after that he gave unto them judges about the
space of four hundred and fifty years, until Samuel the prophet.
21 And afterward they desired a king: and God gave unto them
Saul the son of Cis, a man of the tribe of Benjamin, by the space of
forty years. 22 And when he had removed him, he raised up unto
them David to be their king; to whom also he gave testimony, and
said, I have found David the son of Jesse, a man after mine own
heart, which shall fulfil all my will.

23 Of this man's seed hath God according to his promise raised
unto Israel a Saviour, Jesus: 24 When John had first preached
before his coming the baptism of repentance to all the people of
Israel. (Jesus, the Savior, from the seed of David, as prophesied to
Israel.)

25 And as John fulfilled his course, he said, Whom think ye
that I am? I am not he. But, behold, there cometh one after me,
whose shoes of his feet I am not worthy to loose. 26 Men and
brethren, children of the stock of Abraham, and whosoever among
you feareth God, to you is the word of this salvation sent. (This
message is the saving message, available to all.)

27 For they that dwell at Jerusalem, and their rulers, because they
knew him not, nor yet the voices of the prophets which are read

every sabbath day, they have fulfilled them in condemning him. 28 And though they found no cause of death in him, yet desired they Pilate that he should be slain. (Jesus was an innocent substitute.)

29 And when they had fulfilled all that was written of him, they took him down from the tree, and laid him in a sepulchre. (Jesus fulfilled all the prophecies about Him, according to the scriptures.)

30 But God raised him from the dead: 31 And he was seen many days of them which came up with him from Galilee to Jerusalem, who are his witnesses unto the people. 32 And we declare unto you glad tidings, how that the promise which was made unto the fathers, 33 God hath fulfilled the same unto us their children, in that he hath raised up Jesus again; as it is also written in the second psalm, Thou art my Son, this day have I begotten thee. (This is the "good news," or gospel, that Jesus died on a tree, was buried and physically resurrected, all witnessed. God kept His promises to the Jewish nation. Jesus is God the Son, deity.)

34 And as concerning that he raised him up from the dead, now no more to return to corruption, he said on this wise, I will give you the sure mercies of David. 35 Wherefore he saith also in another psalm, Thou shalt not suffer thine Holy One to see corruption. 36 For David, after he had served his own generation by the will of God, fell on sleep, and was laid unto his fathers, and saw corruption: 37 But he, whom God raised again, saw no corruption. (God's Old Testament title is used, connecting this "good news" with the Jewish scripture. Jesus was sinless and could not be held by death.)

38 Be it known unto you therefore, men and brethren, that through this man is preached unto you the forgiveness of sins: 39 And by him all that believe are justified from all things, from which ye could not be justified by the law of Moses. (Jesus is a real man. Forgiveness from sin is accessed by faith, not by law. Jesus' payment is sufficient for all sins, providing security to those who believe.)

40 Beware therefore, lest that come upon you, which is spoken of in the prophets; 41 Behold, ye despisers, and wonder, and perish: for I work a work in your days, a work which ye shall in no wise believe, though a man declare it unto you. 42 And when the Jews were gone out of the synagogue, the Gentiles besought that these words might be preached to them the next sabbath. (The will of man is moved by urging: persuasion was used to reason with the hearers about the truth of this message.)

43 Now when the congregation was broken up, many of the Jews and religious proselytes followed Paul and Barnabas: who, speaking to them, persuaded them to continue in the grace of God. 44 And the next sabbath day came almost the whole city together to hear the word of God. (Acts 13:15-44)

As important as what Paul's presentation contains, is what it does not contain. False versions of Christianity add to the Gospel works which negate grace. Noteworthy in Acts 13 is that only John's baptism of repentance for Israel is mentioned; water baptism for Christians is not mentioned, required, or practiced, nor is any other human effort, such as verbal declarations, promises to turn from sin, or requests to save. The Gospel of Christ is simply a message to be believed.

The fact that Paul gives a thorough explanation to his hearers does not mean that a person could not be saved by simply hearing the minimal elements of the Gospel, namely the death, burial and resurrection of Jesus Christ for sin. The point is that as Christian witnesses we benefit no one by assuming that a hearer understands the Gospel's elements. What we hope to avoid in witnessing is a situation in which a person is presented an incomplete Gospel and fails to be saved because of a misunderstanding of its elements. As ministers of the Gospel, we believe there is no down-side to thoroughly understanding and explaining the who, what, why, how, and where of the Gospel of Christ, found in 1 Corinthians 15:1-4.

Can't I Just Tell People That Jesus Died for Their Sins?

This chapter detailing salvation is included because of our conviction as authors that many Christians make assumptions not only about the level of understanding of those to whom they witness, but also about the spiritual condition of friends and family, and even fellow church members. There is potential harm in assuming that a person is saved, or that he understands the meaning of the Gospel's elements, while a loving curiosity about the spiritual welfare of others and a willingness to discuss the Gospel is likely to provide many opportunities to glorify God through evangelism and discipleship.

If you have doubts about whether a complete and detailed explanation of the Gospel of Christ is important and necessary, here are some questions you may want to ask yourself:

Could someone be saved if...

...he did not believe that Jesus is God?

...he believed that Jesus is not the only Savior of sinners and the only way to heaven?

...he believed that the source of the Gospel message, the Bible, is not God's word, but was written only by men?

...he thought that the Gospel was an allegory, and not a literal death, burial and resurrection?

...he thought he was "not that bad" or a "good person" rather than a sinner?

...he denied that there is a price to be paid for sinning against God, who is holy and punishes sin?

...he believed that "making a commitment" in response to an altar call, getting baptized by water, "asking Jesus into his heart," or some other religious act saved him? ✓ grace through faith

These questions exemplify commonly held beliefs of many who claim to believe the Gospel. We ask these questions earnestly to encourage Christians to eliminate unnecessary additions, popular shortcuts, and imprecise lingo from their evangelistic efforts, and rather simply explain the elements of 1 Corinthians 15:3-4. Shouldn't we, after all, take God at His word, and present the Gospel by which we are saved?

What does it say about our own beliefs if we think we need to alter or "simplify" God's own message, which He calls the "good news" to mankind? Is there any reason to do so, if it may risk someone's eternal destiny?

The Gospel of Christ reveals who saved us, what He did, why we need it, how we get it, and where we find the information about it. Since God included these facts within His saving message, we believe there is no justification for excluding, changing, or adding to any part of it. Lovingly explaining each element of the Gospel, and helping a hearer to understand its meaning, is the greatest blessing one person can bestow upon another.

CHAPTER 2

WOULD YOU MIND IF I ASKED YOU SOMETHING?

For it is God which worketh in you both to will
and to do of his good pleasure. (Phil 2:13)

Many people we speak with about witnessing tell us that they rarely or never share the gospel, but they want to or believe they should. Some believe they cannot adequately answer the questions which may arise, a need which is addressed in the following chapters of this book. Others say that they do not know how to start the conversation or that they feel intimated by the idea. Still others are worried about causing offense, or about how they will handle a hearer's reaction to a sensitive subject. Concerns such as these can undermine a Christian's confidence in sharing the Gospel. They can keep evangelism from being a positive experience or keep us from doing it at all. If we bring our needs before the Lord, He will work in us to produce both the desire and the ability to do His will (Phil 2:13). He also provides both the desire to know His word and the ability to understand it.

Concerns about sharing the Gospel are perfectly justified. In our politically correct culture, engaging in a discussion about a subject considered controversial may invite rejection or vilification. Simply holding a Biblical world view has, for many Christians, led to personal attack, loss of relationships, and even termination of employment. It is tempting to limit evangelism to extending an invitation to church and hoping that your guest pays attention to the pastor. The church, however, is a body of believers who are all ministers of the Gospel of Christ. The pastor's main calling is to teach believers so that they can mature in the faith (Eph 4:11-12). Part of that maturity is embracing the call to evangelize and walking through the tribulation which may accompany doing so.

Proper motivation is a good starting point for a Christian in his preparation to share the Gospel. Love for our Savior is our motivation to do His will. Sharing the good news is also done out of concern for another person, a sacrifice which was once made for us so that we could be saved. This act of love and obedience is sometimes done for someone who does not appreciate it. We may open ourselves to scorn, mocking, even hatred. Living in a society in which safety, comfort and plenty is so widely available, it may be difficult to get motivated to engage in an activity which may be unpleasant at best. The words of Jesus, Paul and Peter may help us put our fears about evangelism into perspective:

These things I have spoken unto you, that in me ye might have peace. In the world ye shall have tribulation: but be of good cheer; I have overcome the world. (Jn 16:33)

For our light affliction, which is but for a moment, worketh for us a far more exceeding and eternal weight of glory. (2 Cor 4:17)

But the God of all grace, who hath called us unto his eternal glory by Christ Jesus, after that ye have suffered a while, make you perfect, stablish, strengthen, settle you. (1 Pet 5:10)

Approaching evangelism with the mindset described in the previous verses can help us adjust our own expectations, and avoid dejection if we are rebuffed. In addition to proper motivation and an eternal perspective in our expectations, we must access another foundational element of evangelism: faith. We must truly believe that God will equip us. We are all capable of learning and understanding the answers which the Bible provides to answer the objections of hearers. We can do what God asks. He will comfort and sustain us in the face of persecution if that is the result of our evangelistic efforts.

As we consider our daily lives and the various opportunities for evangelism, we may recognize that there are some limitations in our ability to share the Gospel, but there are also occasions when we could, but have not yet made an attempt. If that is so, there is no benefit in guilt or regret, but there is great benefit in responding to the call. Even a trying experience can be a blessing, simply because we trusted God and acted upon His will for us. We can improve the experience for everyone involved if we utilize some self-reflection, and have faith in God's offer to enable us to share His good news with confidence, as well as with gentleness and respect.

The Times I Didn't Speak

As a Christian, I can take the first step in the call to evangelize by evaluating those times when I could have shared something about my faith but chose not to. I may ask myself questions such as:

What held me back? Am I scared, insecure, or intimidated? What did I think would happen if I broached the topic? What am I afraid to lose if it is not well-received?

What kinds of things do I say to myself about witnessing? Do I justify to myself my silence? Is my reluctance about me and my discomfort? Is it about others and their reaction?

Asking oneself questions such as these can shed light on areas for which the grace of God can empower growth. If we are willing to look into what may be holding us back, we can direct our faith toward God's promise that we are thoroughly furnished for ministry. He provides for us both "to will and to do" His good intention for the church, spiritually enabling us with both the ability and the "want to" for evangelism (Phil 2:13; see also 2 Tim 3:16-17, 2 Pet 1:3).

Exposing the Sin Nature

Although the bulk of this book offers biblical answers to objections, a lack of Bible knowledge may be the more easily solved barrier to evangelism. For example, if someone asks me a question that I do not know, I can tell them that I will get back to them later with an answer. But if my poor reaction in a witnessing situation turns it sour, the solution may not be so easy; relationships can be damaged and opportunities lost. Reflecting upon either my evangelism experiences or upon discussions of some other controversial topic, I can evaluate my own feelings and reactions to the experience, and determine how they affected the outcome of the conversation:

What do I recall about how I felt, and how the hearer reacted? Do I remember the experience as a positive one? Did anything I said, did, or felt affect the experience for the better or for the worse? What do I think I need to share the Gospel with confidence?

If someone disagrees with me, do I tend to take offense or feel personally hurt or rejected? If so, how do I then react? Do I, for example, get defensive, or come across like a know-it-all?

If someone tries to argue with me, am I likely to be drawn in, lose my temper, or express exasperation or sarcasm? If I feel annoyed, is it likely to be visible to others?

What are my prejudices? What are my areas of sensitivity? What causes me to over-react?

What tendencies of my sin nature might hinder my ministry efforts?

A little introspection reminds me to bring any counterproductive tendencies I recognize in myself to God, so He may replace them with the virtues of Christ, and a mindset that will best facilitate my ministry. As I direct my faith toward God's provision, He empowers my areas of need. From that place of spiritual strength, I can communicate in a way that provides each hearer with the best environment in which to come to faith in the Gospel of Christ.

Every human being has more inadequacies than he will ever live long enough to realize. These self-evaluation questions are meant to reveal tendencies which we can take to our Lord, knowing He has already provided our victory. Our enemy, however, may use this information to convince us that this endeavor is hopeless. Thoughts of hopelessness, despair, guilt, or other ideas which diminish our position of victory in Christ are signs of attack. If you are under spiritual attack, go to the armor of God, found in Ephesians 6:10-20, to be reminded of your spiritual provisions of truth, righteousness, peace, faith, and salvation in your thinking, and also to meditate upon verses that contradict the attack.

Considering Body Language

For his letters, say they, are weighty and powerful; but his bodily presence is weak, and his speech contemptible. (2 Cor 10:10)

Our inner life is not the only thing to evaluate as we prepare to become witnesses for Christ; our body has a communication system of its own. Consider Paul, who, in order to depend upon the Lord rather than upon his great learnedness and talent for speaking, intentionally spoke simply and plainly, making no effort to personally impress his hearers (1 Cor 2:4). Neither are we as Christians trying to impress others with our own abilities or knowledge. We can look to the example of Paul to help us be mindful of behaviors and habits which may hinder our Gospel presentation.

Most people probably know a little something about body language but have had no reason to evaluate their own. Body language can have a significant effect on communication. A Christian witness may send unintentional messages to hearers or miss an important cue from them in the course of discussing the Gospel or a biblical topic. Discussing a sensitive topic can be trying, and the resulting stress can reveal itself in posture and facial expressions, as well as in the tone, volume, and pacing of our speech. We do not want intimidating or distracting body language to be the impression that we make. Imagine engaging in a conversation that is becoming emotional or otherwise stressful, and ask yourself:

Am I aware of what happens when I become frustrated, anxious or agitated?

Do I speak more quickly or become shrill?

Do I start to raise my voice, commanding the person to whom I am speaking?

Do I lean in, in an intimidating way, or lean back, disengaging?

Do I tend to frown or scowl when someone disagrees with me?

Do I overuse hand gestures, which could seem threatening?

Is my enthusiasm too much, or does my placidity look like disapproval?

Do I notice the body language of others and recognize when it is time to end a conversation?

Gaining and maintaining awareness of body language tendencies can be accomplished by simply talking to yourself in a mirror, or placing a sticky note on your Bible that reads, "tone" or "face," for example. Consider asking a friend about your reactions. He may tell you things that surprise you, but a greater awareness of your presentation style will instill confidence when you share the Gospel.

Exercising Empathy

And such were some of you... (1 Cor 6:11a)

As we evaluate ourselves, the recognition of areas which could use some improvement helps us remember that those with whom we share the Gospel have their issues too. Proactively preparing one's mind with empathy toward those who are "condemned already" can help maintain the attitude and demeanor that is needed to share the love of Christ in the face of potential disagreement and hostility. Hearers of the Gospel may have reasons that we will never know for getting angry or defensive, for avoiding the topic, for disliking the Bible or for rejecting Jesus. Being in a good place with the Lord helps me as a Christian realize that if I share the Gospel of Christ with patience and compassion, a negative reaction is not about me. I can look at the hearer with empathy, knowing that I was once in a similar position. If I, by faith, trust God to produce His fruit in me, I can maintain His peace no matter the outcome (Jn 3:18; Acts 5:41; Phil 1:29, 4:7).

While hostility toward the Gospel is to be expected, there are also those who express no hostility toward it, but after repeated presentations and discussions just do not seem to understand it. Such a hearer may express interest and show willingness, but seem stuck. Feeling angry with oneself for "failing," or feeling exasperated with the hearer can be the result of such an experience. It is important, therefore, to remember that understanding the Gospel of Christ is not a matter of intelligence but of spiritual illumination. You may want to pray that whatever issue is blinding this person will be revealed and removed. Any one of the objections mentioned in this book could keep a person from accepting the Gospel, but it can take time for it to be discovered and answered. Encourage yourself with the reminder that if this person wants to know God, eventually, he will.

Respecting Human Will

...choose you this day whom ye will serve... (Joshua 24:15)

Christians share the Gospel of Christ, found in 1 Corinthians 15:1-4, out of obedience to God and concern for the eternal destiny of souls. We may risk much in order to do so, and yet our message is often disregarded. While refusing the Gospel is a tragedy of eternal consequence, it is God who allows His creatures to reject Him, and it is not part of our calling to give the impression that we are trying to take that choice away. God protects each person's right to exercise freedom, and therefore, as His ministers, we must align ourselves with Him by providing each hearer with the same respect. Respectfulness toward one's personhood is not the same as having respect for his view or his disbelief. It is simply affording him what God already has.

It is helpful to keep in mind that a hearer's refusal may not be final. The word of God is the Spirit's sword; it does its job when we have done ours and proclaimed it. The words of scripture are living and active, and they always accomplish their purpose (Heb 4:12, Isa 55:11). The hearer may need time to give the Gospel message thought and consideration, and may even need to hear it multiple times (Acts 18:4, 19:8, 28:23). The Holy Spirit may need time to work on his mind, convicting him of sin, righteousness, and judgment (Jn 16:8). Sometimes more of life needs to happen; just getting older, and losing things, and losing people may cause one to think differently about eternity. Many people do not care to think about death and what lies beyond until they must face it themselves or deal with the loss of another.

Respecting someone's freedom does not mean that we must smile and nod to everything he says or believes. There is a difference between judging a person and judging doctrine. If a hearer insists, for example, that a Christian doctrine is not true, we can simply reply that the Bible says otherwise, and that he can decide for himself whether or not to believe it. Doing so is not judging him or being disrespectful; it is simply testifying as to what the Bible says. So what does all of this have to do with our personal self-examination? It can be quite painful for us when someone rejects the Gospel, because we know the consequences of rebellion. We need to be alert to the introduction of negative thoughts about God or about His method of saving. Some hearers are experts in their own belief system and can instill doubts in the mind of the Christian witness. Allowing such doubts to take root in our mind can weaken our testimony, damage our Christian life, and lead to bitterness. Therefore, asking ourselves about God's character and plan can help us to prepare for the inevitable refusals we will face. As a Christian witness, I can ask myself questions such as:

Is God my last resort in a trying situation, or do I go first to His word when I have doubts or when I recognize other spiritual attacks?

Can I trust God to continue to lead this person to salvation, and allow myself to let it go if they are not open to the Gospel at this time?

Do I respect the choice God has given this person to reject Him?

Am I likely to fret, obsess, or be upset about a witnessing opportunity that does not end in faith? Do I believe in and use the promise of love, joy, and peace for myself in a difficult or painful situation such as this?

Questions such as these can help us as Christian witnesses realign our thinking with the fact that God desires for all to a come to the knowledge of the truth. He is a good God who is drawing all mankind to Himself through the preaching of the Gospel. A present refusal is not necessarily forever. When we look in faith to the Lord's provision for a good attitude in the face of a refusal, we will grow in our own ability to deal with that disappointment and with other trials as well.

In addition to practicing self-reflection, we can develop or improve communication skills which will smooth the transmission of the Gospel message. As we incorporate these things into our daily interactions and see the results, our confidence in sharing the Gospel will grow as well.

Asking Permission

Religion is considered by many to be very personal; one of the most respectful things we can do is to ask permission to begin a conversation about it. "Would you mind if I asked you something?" is an example of how to open a conversation about any controversial topic. An interaction which allows plenty of breathing room is much more likely to be successful than one which a person feels has been thrust upon him.

Asking permission should also include the option to decline. An example of a question may be, "I was wondering what you think of the Bible." This can be followed by, "I don't mind if you don't want to talk about it." Assuring the hearer that no offense will be taken if he chooses not to discuss the topic is important to preserving whatever relationship you have with this person, or at least showing respect for his feelings if he is someone you do not know. The person who is not interested today may face tragedy tomorrow and realize he has many questions. A respectful initial encounter with you may be the reason he turns to you later when he is ready to talk.

Another matter to consider is the fact that some people believe that it is rude to say, "No." Such a person may agree to talk about his ideas of faith and religion, even if he would rather not. Therefore, a Christian witness should also pay attention to whether or not the hearer appears uncomfortable. For example, is he making eye contact, or is he looking down or away? If a discussion ensues, further permission should be requested. Asking a hearer if he would like to continue talking can protect him from feeling obligated or trapped. A hearer who feels in control of what and how much is discussed may be willing to talk again.

If a detailed conversation does not develop, we need not assume that our efforts failed. Engaging someone does not have to be a major endeavor, but can be a minute or two. In some cases a short conversation is better than a drawn-out discussion. People feel busy, and we do not want them to avoid us later because they assume we are going to talk for an hour. We can plant a seed, pray for them, and watch to see what develops.

Using Qualifying Statements

A qualifying statement is a phrase that softens a request to talk about a sensitive topic. It is also a way to give a hearer an out, or to communicate to him that it is not our intention to be presumptuous, to step on toes, or to be demanding or aggressive. A sincere qualifier such as "you may not agree" or "I may be wrong about this" is intended to convey that you do not wish to cause a feeling of defensiveness. By qualifying, we are not saying that we are wrong about the facts of the Gospel, but rather that we are not making assumptions about the hearer, his beliefs, his level of understanding, or even his interest. We all have expectations, presumptions, biases and other qualities which affect our communication. Maintaining an awareness of these, and letting the hearer know that we are doing so, can help to keep discussions pleasant. As a Christian witness, I want to communicate that in regard to the Bible, I am merely an imperfect person discussing a perfect book.

I do not want to seem like an authority attempting to pressure someone into agreement with me. To this end, qualifying statements work well with asking permission. For example, I might say, "I could be wrong in thinking that you want to learn more. Do you want to continue talking about this?" Communicating in this way lets the hearer know that you respect his time, his feelings, and his right to exit the conversation.

Not Using Leading Questions

Let every man be fully persuaded in his own mind. (Ro 14:5b)

A leading question is one that informs the hearer of the answer you wish to receive. "You know that Jesus is the Savior, right?" "You're a Christian, aren't you?" Questions such as these make it difficult to disagree. The reason that we mention leading questions is because a large number of lost people claim to be Christian. When they are asked a leading question, they know what they are supposed to say. Once a person has expressed agreement with the leading question, it can be difficult to re-open a discussion on the subject in order to determine if he really understood what he affirmed.

Another problem with leading questions is that rushing a conversation to a desired answer can result in a false profession of faith. We must be wary of inadvertently telling a person what to believe. Instead, we should ask him about what he knows already, or what he thinks he knows. We can then compare his response to what scripture teaches about who God is, what He did, why He did it, and how to get it. Doing so provides assurance to both the hearer and the witness that his faith has been placed in something that he really does understand.

If you know someone who has been presented with the Gospel, made a profession, and yet seems not to understand it, you may have seen how difficult this can be for him. Such a person may repeatedly respond to altar calls, re-dedications, or invitations to pray the sinner's prayer, but have no peace or assurance of his salvation. This could be because he does not understand the Gospel. As Christians, we have not accomplished our work if a hearer thinks he is saved because he prayed a prayer, accepted an altar invitation, or answered a leading question in a certain way. Instead, we want to help him be certain that he is a Christian because the Gospel is true and he believes it, and not for any other reason. In witnessing, we are not selling him anything. We are not simply trying to "get a yes." We are providing truths to be understood, so that each hearer will come to believe the Gospel of Christ by which we are saved, found in 1 Corinthians 15:1-4.

Asking Rather Than Telling

He said to them, 'But who do you say that I am? (Mt 16:15 NASB)

Although leading questions are not helpful in witnessing, asking questions is a very good way to open communication about the Gospel. Non-Christians may expect Christian witnesses to make pushy pronouncements and tell them what they are supposed to think. If we instead look for opportunities to ask others about their beliefs, we can better understand their viewpoint, and recognize potential objections to the Gospel. Using that knowledge, we can guide a hearer to Biblical answers about his particular concerns, rather than forcing a discussion into a pre-set formula.

Asking, of course, is not grilling someone, but politely inquiring to learn more about what he already understands or believes. Saying, "I was wondering if you would be willing to tell me what you think of Christianity," is an invitation to the hearer to talk freely about his ideas and beliefs, while retaining the option to not answer. If a conversation ensues, it should not feel like a quiz. Initially, you may just listen, offering no opinion or correction unless asked. A hearer's feeling of security in discussing a sensitive topic will ideally facilitate further discussions about God, the Bible, or any doubts he has about a false religious system with which he may be involved.

Not Asking for a "Decision"

And when he is come, he will reprove the world of sin,
and of righteousness, and of judgment... (Jn 16:8)

While a question may be a good beginning to a discussion of the Gospel, it may not be the best way to end it. Having presented someone with the Gospel of Christ, it is understandably rewarding to know that he has believed. Some Christians have been taught to ask a hearer to "make a decision for Christ" at the close of a conversation about the Gospel. Such a strategy, however well-intentioned, can be problematic, because the witness may be inadvertently putting the hearer on the spot. Believing that he is expected to come to faith right then, the hearer may feel pressure to give a positive response, although he has not had time to consider what he has heard or to formulate questions. He may make a declaration of faith in order to please us. He may even say, "Yes," simply to get rid of us!

41

Furthermore, some of the phraseology used to bring this person to a decision may not contain the Gospel by which we are saved. A person can claim to "follow Jesus," without believing the Gospel of Christ. He can pray the "sinner's prayer" without understanding its elements; he can "make a decision for Jesus" without being born again. We believe that nearly any person, having given it some thought, will have some objection to the Gospel. It is safer to allow a hearer some time to consider what he has heard than to put him on the spot to decide what he believes. That does not mean, however, that a hearer cannot articulate with proper understanding the elements of the Gospel and be saved upon hearing it. The point is to avoid setting the stage for a false conversion.

The risk of a false conversion in an unconvinced person creates another problem. If at some future time he is recognized as someone who does not understand the Gospel, it can be difficult to re-open the discussion. Having been told that when he prayed a prayer of salvation, he was saved if he "really meant it," he may be unlikely to be open to the Gospel again. Becoming a Christian requires nothing more than being convinced of the truth of the Gospel of Christ. Asking someone to do or say something invites the risk of transferring the hearer's faith to the suggested act, rather than placing it in the Gospel message. It is imperative that we recognize the danger in making such a suggestion, one which may distract his mind when the Holy Spirit is doing His work of convincing.

In our experience as Christian witnesses, we have found that many people do not even know what they believe. They have not thought deeply about the Gospel nor heard it explained fully. If we, as Christian witnesses, share whatever amount of truth a person is willing to hear and ask if we can follow up with him later, then we can leave our efforts with the Lord and with prayer. The hearer may come back to us with more questions, or he may ask someone else a decade from now. We may never know if he came to believe, but we can have confidence in both God's time line and in His efforts to save.

Not Investing in the Immediate Outcome

I have planted, Apollos watered; but God gave the increase. (1 Cor 3:6)

It may seem like a contradiction to suggest that a Christian avoid getting invested in whether someone believes the Gospel or rejects it. We would not be witnesses if we did not care. But focusing on one's personal investment in the process, as opposed to an attitude of resting in the Lord's plan, can evoke emotions which might undermine the process. For example, the hearer may be someone I want very much to be saved, and if he rejects the Gospel, it may trigger emotions in me which may negatively impact the conversation or even the relationship, closing the door to further discussion of the Gospel. Not only can an over-investment rob me of the joy in having done God's will, in the long term, it could become bitterness. If I, as a Christian witness, find myself angry, insulted, depressed or discouraged after witnessing, those feelings may be a result of focusing on the response of the hearer, or on critiquing my own skill in witnessing, rather than on the joy of sharing God's good news.

If my focus is on the character of God and on His desire that the lost should be saved, I can place my confidence in Him, trusting His timing and His work in their hearts. I know that His Holy Spirit will be ministering the truths I shared. The spiritual journey of those with whom I share the

Gospel is not about me. My investment must be in obeying God, not in whether someone gets saved on my watch. I can then look upon the opportunity to share in His work with thankfulness and enjoy His peace.

Keeping it About the Bible

But avoid foolish questions, and genealogies, and contentions, and strivings about the law; for they are unprofitable and vain. (Titus 3:9)

A similar temptation to being emotionally invested in the outcome of witnessing is the craving to be proven right. Salvation can be a highly charged subject, and sometimes what begins with good intentions turns into a competitive sport. It is not easy to be told we are wrong, naive, or gullible for any reason, but to be ridiculed for believing God can be the epitome of aggravation. The irony of it all is that this critic is someone whom we are trying to bless. It is easy to become exasperated and to think to oneself, "Well, that's it! Now I'm just going to prove you wrong!"

In order to preserve the opportunity to discuss the Gospel further, we must resist challenging the hearer, or allowing him to "push our buttons." We need to recognize the rise of defensiveness within ourselves, and the triggers which can draw us into a fruitless debate. Our good judgment, our intelligence, or some other quality may be under attack, but nonetheless, we must try to return the conversation to the issues surrounding the Gospel rather than being drawn into a duel. If we keep the conversation Bible-centered, it is easier to remind ourselves and the hearer that his argument is not with us; it is with God.

In many cases, keeping the conversation on track is not easy. Even those who are best-equipped with scriptural answers can be bested by clever people with quick retorts. It helps to remember the big picture of what we as Christians are trying to achieve. For example, if someone thinks I am wrong, so what? This is not a contest. If the hearer feels better about getting the last word, so be it. It is better to let him "win," than to answer back and risk damaging my credibility. In order to consider my testimony, he needs to see me as reasonable rather than reactive, and as someone who is willing to listen to his thoughts and feelings. If I allow the conversation to degrade, I may reinforce the politically correct norm that no one should "talk religion."

If you think you went too far by getting emotional, defensive, or pushy, or if you suspect that the hearer feels wronged, be quick to apologize. Spiritual forces are at work against each of us, accusing us, and endeavoring to stop the conversations we have with the lost. As evangelists, we must keep pointing back to the Bible and away from ourselves so that we do not inadvertently make ourselves sound like the best reason to reject salvation.

Bowing Out Gracefully

The Gospel of Christ is an offense to a world in rebellion. As we evangelize, we are not to remove the offense of the Gospel, but we are to avoid being an offense ourselves. The power of the Spirit within us can produce patience, a right attitude, and a loving demeanor as we testify to the truth of the Gospel, even if the hearer is offended by its message. A hearer who becomes angry may be experiencing conviction by the Holy Spirit. If we have not been offensive in our presentation, a hearer's reaction is not about us. If we do not bow out, however, the situation could become about us. Continuing to try to reason with an angry or defensive person is unlikely to be fruitful. In such a situation, we need to place our faith in the promise of James 1:5, which teaches that God provides us with ample wisdom. We can then decide if it is best to end the conversation, at least for the present time.

If emotions are rising, acknowledge that fact, and let the hearer know that your intention is not to offend. It may help to empathize with his viewpoint, to assure him that you know his beliefs are his own choice, and to remind him that the scriptures are the authority, not you. Communicating these things may diffuse the emotion so the discussion can be ended amicably.

Because we want those around us to know the love of God in Christ Jesus, protecting our relationships and the opportunity to talk further is one of our goals as evangelists. Another goal is to avoid reinforcing the "no-talk" rule about religion, which maintains the gag order on Christians and non-Christians alike. If the conversation does not end well, remember that rejection is not necessarily forever. Other opportunities may well arise. Another point to keep in mind, especially for the over-achievers and perfectionists among us, is that God's love for us is not outcome-based; it is gracious.

Knowing It and Saying It Are Different

Remember that job interview, when you had these great things to say about your work experience, but when you started talking, it did not come out as you had imagined? Have you ever taken an oral examination and realized how different it is to explain something than it is to read about it? Developing the practice of talking about truth makes it feel as natural as talking about work or the weather. Practice explaining the Gospel to a friend, or share with your spouse what you read during your devotional time. Incorporate what you learn into your prayer life by telling God the wonderful things that you know about Him. In short, talk about truth.

Speaking aloud has another advantage: it aids memory. For example, when we hear a sermon, take notes, look up the verses, and talk about what we learned, we experience four times the exposure to those truths. If you practice talking about the Gospel in a situation that does not intimidate you, then you may find it is easier to do the same on other occasions. As you incorporate additional communication skills and greater-self awareness into your evangelism efforts, always directing your faith toward the Lord for His enabling, you will find yourself sharing the Gospel with confidence!

My Christian Life is My Life!

... ye shine as lights in the world; Holding forth the word of life...
(Phil 2:15b-16a)

Some of us were introduced to church as a Sunday activity which had nothing to do with the rest of our lives. We appeared, sat quietly, read the words when prompted, and left. "Church" had no relevance nor impact on our daily living. Having been born again, we now know that our faith includes so much more. As we mature, we find that nothing in life exists apart from our relationship with our Lord. Christianity is not part of our life, it is our life.

Some, however, find it is difficult to incorporate Christianity into everyday life. One's faith may be segregated from other parts of life and rarely mentioned. Trying to imagine talking about it with friends might seem awkward, let alone with strangers. If this lack of incorporation is simply a habit, or due to being busy or single-minded, something as simple as a sticky note or an electronic alarm can reminds us to "check in with God." Taking a moment to pray, to mention a truth of scripture to someone, or to share the Gospel, are all ways in which we allow the mind of Christ to flow through our everyday life. We can teach ourselves to keep God involved in our day, integrating faith into our ordinary routine, and gradually making it more natural to mention a little truth to others. Because God created the universe, and His truth is intended to inform our every word and action, no topic is beyond the realm of Biblical relevance. Realizing this can open many doors to incorporating our faith into daily life.

In summary, as a Christian, I can prepare myself to evangelize by aligning my will with God's will, confidently sharing the Gospel out of love and a desire to obey God's call. I can reflect upon the experiences I have had in evangelistic situations, and on the times when I declined to speak. I can evaluate my style of interacting with others, and the attitudes I have toward those who disagree with me. I can recognize and improve the characteristics of my communication, and practice using them. I can learn the Gospel thoroughly and read the Bible regularly, so that God's words are in my mind and on my tongue. All these things are part of my personal growth as a witness for Jesus Christ.

A spiritual mindset and an improved way of communicating is not ultimately about methods, however, but about cultivating a view of evangelism which incorporates our eternal life naturally into our earthly one. Christians know that we are to share the Gospel with boldness. The development of a bold and confident attitude is facilitated by the removal of those things which we feel hold us back. It is easier to be bold when you have ready responses to objections, and some level of certainty that you can present the Gospel without causing offense.

As you begin to view your ministry efforts as less about gaining converts and more about determining who is interested in and open to God, the Bible, or salvation, you may find that there is less pressure on both you and on the hearer when a conversation arises. Such a view of evangelism helps to avoid false conversions, because we are talking to someone we are concerned about, rather than trying to get the answer we want. It also keeps our interactions with others natural and unforced. As evangelists, we are sharing in the Lord's work, not "working a program." We are holding forth something to the world, not trying to get them to do something for us. We can improve our efforts, and yet hold loosely to them, because we are resting in the gracious provision of our Savior God, our partner in the work of the ministry.

Redeeming the Time

Walk in wisdom toward them that are without,
redeeming the time. (Col 4:5)

In this chapter we have looked at areas for personal reflection, and suggestions for communication which can smooth our presentation of the Gospel. In addition to these ideas for personal growth, there is a big picture for us to consider. This big picture is seen when we look up from the grocery list in the store aisle, from the waiting room magazine, the pile on our desk, or the apple of our eye. There are lost people all around us. Sometimes hearing an interesting comment or conversation is an opportunity to interject a tidbit of truth. It may not be about the Gospel at all, but it may be a starting point to show, for example, that I am a "safe" person with whom to discuss sensitive topics, the Bible, or religion in general. I may be the only person. I may have only a minute, but God can make use of it if I will.

A positive interaction may provide a future opportunity to share or answer questions. Redeeming the time does not mean that we necessarily press forward to share as much as possible, but only that we say something, whatever we comfortably can. As we pay attention to the hearer's reaction, and remain willing to drop the conversation, we can make good use of an opportunity to say a word about God or the Bible, without pushing it too far.

Whether you are quoting a Bible verse, mentioning a biblical principle, or simply making your position known on a subject which is impacted by your faith, your comment may be well-received, ignored, or rebuffed. A seed is planted when the opportunity is taken to display knowledge of the Bible, a willingness to talk about it, and a lack of antipathy toward the other person's beliefs. By doing so, a Christian can redeem even a small moment of time for God's glorious purpose.

But ye, brethren, be not weary in well doing. (2 Thes 3:13)

...our sufficiency is of God; Who also hath made us able ministers... (2 Co 3:5b-6a)

CHAPTER 3

WHO HE IS

God and the Person of Jesus Christ

For in him dwelleth all the fullness of the Godhead bodily. (Col 2:9)

The Gospel of Christ, found in 1 Corinthians 15:1-4, contains five elements which can be identified as who, what, why, how and where. All five tell us something about Jesus Christ, God the Son. Jesus is the one who died on a cross. He died as a sacrifice for sin because every person is born in need of salvation from sin. Salvation is accessed by faith in His work on the cross for sins, and the source of these truths is the Bible, the revelation of Jesus Christ to mankind.

Because Jesus and His work on the cross is the object of our faith for salvation, who Jesus is must necessarily be central to the Gospel message. Objections to "who He is" may be in regard to Jesus in particular or to God in general, such as to God's triune nature, His attributes, or His character. Some take issue with Jesus' deity, considering Him a sort of "God-Junior," or merely a created being. Others do not recognize the differences between the God of the Bible and the deities of false religion, the movies, or their own imaginations.

Those who believe the record of the Bible know who God is. They believe the testimony of Israel's prophets, who proclaimed that God was their Savior. The New Testament identified to the world that God the Savior was the man Jesus of Nazareth. Believing in a false God or a false Jesus does not save. This chapter responds to objections to who He is.

"Jesus isn't God! He was just..."
(a teacher, a prophet, a good man)

And Thomas answered and said unto Him, My Lord and my God.
(Jn 20:28)

A common objection to Jesus Christ is to deny that He is fully God, and one of the three divine persons who comprise the Godhead. Some consider Jesus a lesser being, a created being, or simply a man who was a moral teacher or a prophet. This is not the message of scripture, which reveals that Israel's Savior is God:

> *Yet I am the LORD thy God from the land of Egypt, and thou shalt know no god but me: for there is no saviour beside me.*
> (Hos 13:4)

John tells us that the Word, a title for Jesus Christ, is the Creator and is God:

> *In the beginning was the Word, and the Word was with God, and the Word was God. The same was in the beginning with God. All things were made by him; and without him was not any thing made that was made.* (Jn 1:1-3)

Jesus' statement that He is one with the Father was a claim to be God. This was perfectly clear to the Jews, who were enraged by it:

> *I and my Father are one. Then the Jews took up stones again to stone him. Jesus answered them, Many good works have I shewed you from my Father; for which of those works do ye stone me?*

The Jews answered him, saying, For a good work we stone thee not; but for blasphemy; and because that thou, being a man, makest thyself God. (Jn 10:30-33)

Jesus did things that God would do. He performed miracles such as commanding the elements; He accepted worship, and He forgave sins:

And he saith unto them, Why are ye fearful, O ye of little faith? Then he arose, and rebuked the winds and the sea; and there was a great calm. But the men marvelled, saying, What manner of man is this, that even the winds and the sea obey him! (Mt 8:26-27)

And as they went to tell his disciples, behold, Jesus met them, saying, All hail. And they came and held him by the feet, and worshipped him. (Mt 28:9)

Whether is it easier to say to the sick of the palsy, Thy sins be forgiven thee; or to say, Arise, and take up thy bed, and walk? (Mk 2:9)

In addition to His words and deeds, Jesus' birth, ministry, and death fulfilled hundreds of Biblical prophecies. Among them is one which calls his name Immanuel, meaning, "God with us."

Therefore the Lord himself shall give you a sign; Behold, a virgin shall conceive, and bear a son, and shall call his name Immanuel. (Isa 7:14)

Colossians contains one of the most descriptive passages about the deity of Jesus Christ, describing Him as the Savior from sin, the very likeness of God, and the eternal Creator. Speaking of God the Father, and Jesus, who is God the Son, Paul writes:

> *Who hath delivered us from the power of darkness, and hath translated us into the kingdom of his dear Son: In whom we have redemption through his blood, even the forgiveness of sins: Who is the image of the invisible God, the firstborn of every creature: For by him were all things created, that are in heaven, and that are in earth, visible and invisible, whether they be thrones, or dominions, or principalities, or powers: all things were created by him, and for him: And he is before all things, and by him all things consist. And he is the head of the body, the church: who is the beginning, the firstborn from the dead; that in all things he might have the preeminence.* (Col 1:13-18)

Jesus declared Himself, "I am," a reference to His self-existent nature. This is the name God revealed to Moses, the father of the nation of Israel:

> *And God said unto Moses, I AM THAT I AM: and he said, Thus shalt thou say unto the children of Israel, I AM hath sent me unto you.* (Ex 3:14)

> *That is why I told you that you will die in your sins, for unless you believe that I AM, you'll die in your sins.* (Jn 8:24 ISV)

> *I'm telling you this now, before it happens, so that when it does happen, you may believe that I AM.* (Jn 13:19 ISV)

Jesus said unto them, Verily, verily, I say unto you, Before Abraham was, I am. (Jn 8:58)

Jesus is a man, but He is not merely a man. The testimony of scripture is that Jesus is God the Son, the Creator, the I AM, and the fulfillment of the Old Testament prophecies that a savior would come.

"God is not a trinity. The word isn't even in the Bible."

...in the name of the Father, and the Son, and the Holy Spirit... (Mt 28:19b NASB)

Although the word "trinity" is not in the Bible, it does describe a biblical concept. This doctrine is denied by many non-Christians, but there are probably few who could raise a lucid objection to it. Similarly, it is likely that few Christians could defend the tri-unity of God by explaining it, so do not feel that you need to be a "Trinity expert" in order to effectively share the Gospel.

In your witnessing efforts, you may encounter someone trained to refute the Trinity, who could draw you into a fruitless battle with this complex objection. Anti-trinitarian religions masquerading as Christian are willing to invest hours, and even weeks or months working toward the goal of converting a person to their belief. Sharing a few applicable verses will probably be sufficient to reveal whether or not the objector is willing to consider this doctrine.

Some denials of the Trinity are based on the claim that God is a singular entity who has three roles or forms. Such an explanation does not hold up when members of the Godhead make references to one another:

> *A little while, and ye shall not see me: and again, a little while, and ye shall see me, because I go to the Father.* (Jn 16:16)

> *But the Comforter, which is the Holy Ghost, whom the Father will send in my name, he shall teach you all things, and bring all things to your remembrance, whatsoever I have said unto you.* (Jn 14:26)

> *But when the Comforter is come, whom I will send unto you from the Father, even the Spirit of truth, which proceedeth from the Father, he shall testify of me...* (Jn 15:26)

> *And lo a voice from heaven, saying, This is my beloved Son, in whom I am well pleased.* (Mt 3:17)

Also supporting the doctrine of the Trinity are passages which make reference to all three persons in the Godhead:

> *Elect according to the foreknowledge of God the Father, through sanctification of the Spirit, unto obedience and sprinkling of the blood of Jesus Christ: Grace unto you, and peace, be multiplied.* (1 Pet 1:2)

> *And be not drunk with wine, wherein is excess; but be filled with the Spirit; Speaking to yourselves in psalms and hymns and spiritual songs, singing and making melody in your heart*

to the Lord; Giving thanks always for all things unto God and the Father in the name of our Lord Jesus Christ. (Eph 5:18-20)

For through him we both have access by one Spirit unto the Father. (Eph 2:18)

Come ye near unto me, hear ye this; I have not spoken in secret from the beginning; from the time that it was, there am I: and now the Lord GOD, and his Spirit, hath sent me. Thus saith the LORD, thy Redeemer, the Holy One of Israel; I am the LORD thy God which teacheth thee to profit, which leadeth thee by the way that thou shouldest go. (Isa 48:16-17)

For unto us a child is born, unto us a son is given: and the government shall be upon his shoulder: and his name shall be called Wonderful, Counsellor, The mighty God, The everlasting Father, The Prince of Peace. (Isa 9:6)

A subtle revelation of the Trinity can be found in the biblical use of pronouns, such as in Genesis Chapter 1. When Moses refers to God, he uses the singular words "his" and "he." When describing the persons of God communicating amongst themselves, the plural "us" is used:

*And God said, Let **us** make man in **our** image, after **our** likeness: and let them have dominion over the fish of the sea, and over the fowl of the air, and over the cattle, and over all the earth, and over every creeping thing that creepeth upon the earth. So God created man in **his** own image, in the image of God created **he** him; male and female created **he** them."* (Gen 1:26-27, emphasis added)

It is difficult to describe the Trinity because there is nothing and no one else like God, but it can help to compare Him to something we understand, such as humankind. We will refer to the kind of being that God is as "God-kind."

There is only one being that can be classified as God-kind; there is no other like Him. If we compare the substance of God-kind with that of humankind, we know that humankind exists in an individual human body which is made of matter. God-kind, however, is spirit. Spirit is what He is made of; it is the substance of His being.

God reveals Himself as being one and also as existing in three persons. When God is described as being one, it means that He is one spirit, the only one of His kind. God-kind is also a trinity, referring to the fact that three persons share one spirit. The persons of God are not separate individuals as are humans, who exist independently from one another. God is unique: one God in three persons.

The unity of God, meaning that God is one spirit, is taught in scripture:

> *And Jesus answered him, The first of all the commandments is, Hear, O Israel; The Lord our God is one Lord...* (Mk 12:29)

> *Thou believest that there is one God; thou doest well: the devils also believe, and tremble.* (Jas 2:19)

> *God is Spirit: and those who worship him must worship in spirit and truth.* (Jn 4:24 NSAB)

Additional support for the Trinity is that all three divine persons are called "God." The Father is God:

Blessed be God, even the Father of our Lord Jesus Christ, the Father of mercies, and the God of all comfort. (2 Cor 1:3)

And that every tongue should confess that Jesus Christ is Lord, to the glory of God the Father. (Phil 2:11)

The second person of the Trinity, the Son, is God:

In the beginning was the Word, and the Word was with God, and the Word was God. (Jn 1:1)

For in him dwelleth all the fullness of the Godhead bodily. (Col 2:9)

The third person of the Trinity, the Holy Spirit, is God:

But Peter said, Ananias, why hath Satan filled thine heart to lie to the Holy Ghost, and to keep back part *of the price of the land? Whiles it remained, was it not thine own? and after it was sold, was it not in thine own power? why hast thou conceived this thing in thine heart? thou hast not lied unto men, but unto God.* (Acts 5:3-4)

The Spirit of the Lord spake by me, and his word was in my tongue. (2 Sam 23:2)

Any one of the aforementioned aspects of God or several them may be needed to answer the questions of hearers about God. As witnesses of the Gospel of Christ, we can allow the Bible to speak for itself to describe Him. Doing so allows each hearer to decide for himself if he believes the biblical record.

"The Bible has two different gods: an angry, punitive god in the Old Testament, and a kind and forgiving Jesus in the New Testament. These cannot be the same God, so I don't believe."

For I am the LORD, I change not... (Mal 3:6a)

Using an unbalanced portrayal of God in the Bible, some objectors claim that the God described in the Old Testament is different than Jesus. Seeming differences, however, only reflect the various aspects of God's character shown throughout scripture. That God is not one-dimensional is apparent when the whole counsel of scripture is considered. In an attempt to distinguish Jesus in the New Testament from God in the Old Testament, objectors characterize Him as passive and mild, but He sometimes expressed righteous anger:

> *And they come to Jerusalem: and Jesus went into the temple, and began to cast out them that sold and bought in the temple, and overthrew the tables of the moneychangers, and the seats of them that sold doves; And would not suffer that any man should carry any vessel through the temple. And he taught, saying unto them, Is it not written, My house shall be called of all nations the house of prayer? But ye have made it a den of thieves!* (Mk 11:15-17)

Selectively using Old Testament verses, objectors accuse God of being angry and punitive. On the contrary, His dealings with Adam and Eve, those of Noah's time, the people of Ninevah, and rebellious Israel belie this characterization. Psalm 145 contains one of many beautiful Old

Testament tributes to God's character amid the repeated failings of His chosen nation Israel:

The LORD is gracious, and full of compassion; slow to anger, and of great mercy. The LORD is good to all: and his tender mercies are over all his works. (Ps 145:8-9)

God's character is perfectly balanced. He is kind, loving, patient, and merciful toward mankind. He is also just and always does rightly, which includes dispensing just punishment. Because God is teaching mankind different lessons at various times in history, some Bible portions put a greater emphasis on a particular aspect of God's character. An example of one of God's lessons to humanity is that He is holy and we are sinful. Referring to the Law of Moses, Paul explains God's purpose in administrating Israel with a legal system:

Therefore by the deeds of the law there shall no flesh be justified in his sight: for by the law is the knowledge of sin. (Ro 3:20)

Under God's perfect law system, the failings of man were made clear, thereby displaying the holiness of God in contrast. Providing evidence that humanity is sinful was meant to illuminate man's need for a savior. When the Savior came, John tells us that Jesus' ministry had a different purpose than did the Law:

For the law was given by Moses, but grace and truth came by Jesus Christ. (Jn 1:17)

Jesus' ministry was to display God's grace, culminating in His death on a cross to pay for the sins of the world. In the New Testament, we do not see a different god, or a change in God; what we see is a new chapter in God's plan and a new administration over His people. For Christians, recognizing the unfolding revelation within the Bible is crucial to both rightly understanding it and explaining it to hearers. Those who believe that the Bible contradicts itself in describing who God is can be shown His unfolding plan and the various facets of His holy character.

"God is love, and a loving God would not send anyone to hell."

And in hell he lift up his eyes, being in torments, and seeth Abraham afar off, and Lazarus in his bosom. (Lk 16:23)

In some cases, an objection to who God is, is due to a misunderstanding of His good character. Denying the consequence of sin is an example of this because it denies God's holiness. Objecting to hell by protesting that "God is love" misses the point that failing to judge sin is the equivalent of approving of it. Yes, God is love, but He is also just, always acting rightly. A human judge who let a convicted murderer go unpunished would not be considered to be performing an act of love, but one of corruption for failing to dispense justice. Because God's character is balanced between His loving kindness and His holy justice, He cannot ignore sin. Therefore, He has provided a solution to the problem of sin which is free, available to all, and recorded in the Gospel of Christ, 1 Corinthians 15:1-4. An objector who believes in a one-sided god does not believe in the righteous God of the Bible.

God's holiness was on display under the Law of Moses, which clearly and continually revealed God's high expectations and the sinful failings of mankind:

And Joshua said unto the people, Ye cannot serve the LORD: for he is an holy God; he is a jealous God; he will not forgive your transgressions nor your sins. If ye forsake the LORD, and serve strange gods, then he will turn and do you hurt, and consume you, after that he hath done you good. (Josh 24:19-20)

Sanctify yourselves therefore, and be ye holy: for I am the LORD your God. And ye shall keep my statutes, and do them: I am the LORD which sanctify you. (Lev 20:7-8)

God asked His people to act in accordance with His holiness, but their disobedience revealed the need for a savior from sin. In the New Testament, the Savior was provided, and God's grace was displayed:

And the Word was made flesh, and dwelt among us, (and we beheld his glory, the glory as of the only begotten of the Father,) full of grace and truth (Jn 1:14)

For the law was given by Moses, but grace and truth came by Jesus Christ. (Jn 1:17)

If we confess our sins, he is faithful and just to forgive us our sins, and to cleanse us from all unrighteousness. (1 Jn 1:9)

The Gospel shows God's provision to satisfy both His holiness and His love for mankind. His holiness was satisfied by pouring out the punishment for sin upon a substitute for mankind, the person of Jesus Christ. God's love was satisfied by offering to all mankind a payment for sins, a gift which is available through by faith in the death, burial and resurrection of Jesus Christ. Perhaps the hearer who objects to hell has not considered that he is counting his own mercy and judgment to be superior to God's, or that he is attacking the record of the Bible and the honesty of Jesus, who spoke of hell many times and died to save us from it. Jesus is God in the flesh. He was not misinformed or lying when he warned his listeners of judgment to come:

> *And if thy right hand offend thee, cut it off, and cast it from thee: for it is profitable for thee that one of thy members should perish, and not that thy whole body should be cast into hell.* (Mt 5:30)

> *Ye serpents, ye generation of vipers, how can ye escape the damnation of hell?* (Mt 23:33)

Because of who He is, God will ultimately provide justice for all. Because of God's love and mercy, He has also provided a solution to the problem of sin. His desire is that none should perish but rather that all should come to repentance (2 Pet 3:9). As Christian witnesses, we can help hearers to recognize that hell is the selection that each person makes when he rejects the provision of God for his eternal destiny.

"There is too much suffering and evil in the world. I reject a God who allows it!"

These things I have spoken unto you, that in me ye might have peace. In the world ye shall have tribulation: but be of good cheer; I have overcome the world. (Jn 16:33)

A hearer who objects to the Gospel because of the world's suffering is not seeing God as good, perhaps because of painful losses of his own. Gently inquiring about whether that is the case may be a good place to start. Without the Biblical perspective to reveal the "big picture" of life, this world can seem to offer little more than pain, disappointment, and fleeting happiness. As Christians, we have a hope beyond this world which is a comfort to us. Those who see no solution to the world's troubles may see God as heartless, and Christians as escapists who only want to dream of heaven and not fix this earth. They do not yet understand that believing the Gospel *is* the solution, freeing us from sin and death. As we share who God is, a hearer may be willing to consider the Bible's response to suffering.

To explain suffering and evil, a Christian witness may want to include its cause, beginning with the fall of Adam and Eve, covered in Chapter 1. The objection, however, is really an expression of doubt regarding God's goodness. God is the easy target of blame for the world's troubles, but He is not the cause. Suffering did not exist when God created the earth; what He created was good:

And God saw everything that he had made, and, behold, it was very good. (Gen 1:31a)

Our good God not only provides for His children; He even provides for those who reject Him:

That ye may be the children of your Father which is in heaven: for he maketh his sun to rise on the evil and on the good, and sendeth rain on the just and on the unjust. (Mt 5:45)

God helps His children when asked. He offers a moral code that, when followed, allows us to avoid many calamities. He fulfills prophecy so that we know He always keeps His word.

And this is the confidence that we have in him, that, if we ask any thing according to his will, he heareth us... (1 Jn 5:14)

And we know that all things work together for good to them that love God, to them who are the called according to his purpose. (Ro 8:28)

For whatsoever things were written aforetime were written for our learning, that we through patience and comfort of the scriptures might have hope. (Ro 15:4)

Some of the earth's problems are due to the curse of sin. God did curse the earth (Gen 3:17-19), but He also provided a solution to sin and a future free from its evils:

And God shall wipe away all tears from their eyes; and there shall be no more death, neither sorrow, nor crying, neither shall there be any more pain: for the former things are passed away. (Rev 21:4)

The earth is sin-cursed because the first two people rejected God's wise counsel. Therefore, even the problems that are not directly caused by man today were indirectly caused by man. It was Adam who sinned, and we would all do the same; we would act independently from God and disobey Him, because everyone less than God will act less than godly. Much of this world's suffering continues to be caused by man, and is done in opposition to God's will:

> *And GOD saw that the wickedness of man* was *great in the earth, and* that *every imagination of the thoughts of his heart* was *only evil continually. And it repented the LORD that he had made man on the earth, and it grieved him at his heart.* (Gen 6:5-6)

Humanity is fallen and sinful, perpetrating many evils. It can be frustrating when things seem unfair, but God is just, and nobody will "get away" with anything:

> *Dearly beloved, avenge not yourselves, but* rather *give place unto wrath: for it is written, Vengeance* is *mine; I will repay, saith the Lord.* (Ro 12:19)

The issue of suffering returns us to the matter of God's character, and specifically to whether or not He is good. The evidence that He is good can be seen in the hope He offers for our future. The biblical meaning of hope is to have a confident expectation:

> *For God sent not his Son into the world to condemn the world; but that the world through him might be saved.* (Jn 3:17)

But I would not have you to be ignorant, brethren, concerning them which are asleep, that ye sorrow not, even as others which have no hope. (1 Thess 4:13)

Now the God of hope fill you with all joy and peace in believing, that ye may abound in hope, through the power of the Holy Ghost. (Ro 15:13)

In hope of eternal life, which God, that cannot lie, promised before the world began. (Titus 1:2)

Blessed be the God and Father of our Lord Jesus Christ, which according to his abundant mercy hath begotten us again unto a lively hope by the resurrection of Jesus Christ from the dead... (1 Pet 1:3)

Wherefore gird up the loins of your mind, be sober, and hope to the end for the grace that is to be brought unto you at the revelation of Jesus Christ... (1 Pet 1:13)

If we look away from the calamities of this world and acknowledge that much of what happens in this life is not according to God's will, we can place our confident expectation in Him. God's word tells us who He is, assuring a perfect eternity to all who believe Him. Yes, there is suffering in the world, but by believing the Gospel of Christ, we have surety and hope for our future (1 Cor 15:1-4). It is this message that we wish to convey to hearers who object to God because they blame Him for the world's suffering.

"I believe in...

...something like the 'Star Wars force' with a dark and light side."

...the God of my own understanding."

...some kind of higher power."

...well, not the God of the Bible."

That at the name of Jesus every knee should bow, of things in heaven, and things in earth, and things under the earth; And that every tongue should confess that Jesus Christ is Lord, to the glory of God the Father. (Phil 2:10-11)

Considering the wide variety of ideas about who God is, it is not surprising that Jesus said many people will believe anything except the truth:

> *And **because** I tell you the truth, ye believe me not.* (Jn 8:45, emphasis added)

An impersonal force that can be used to accomplish things is a popular idea about who God is. The "Star Wars force," for example, can be used for good or evil, depending upon who wields it. Nature is a kind of god to some, but nature has no personality; you can't have a relationship with forces of nature. Tribal gods are unpredictable and untrustworthy. Mohammed, the founder of Islam, made his tribal god, Allah, the god of a new religion. But Allah has no concern for his followers. He is wicked, unjust and not at all merciful. His followers cannot count on him and never know what to expect from him. The God of the Bible is both personal and concerned for all mankind.

Despite the differences among various religions regarding who God is, they all teach some standard of behavior or have rules to follow. With a standard comes the need for a judge who must determine if followers meet the standard. But only a personal God can be a judge; neither nature nor a "force" can make moral determinations. Only a person has a conscience and can know right from wrong. The God of the Bible is more than a judge; He is a righteous judge. He calls us to use reason and to display virtue. The scriptures testify that the character of the true God, Jehovah, is goodness and love, kindness and grace, reason and justice, help and hope. He is a personal God, and we can know Him, trust Him, and have a relationship with Him:

> *And I will give them an heart to know me, that I am the LORD: and they shall be my people, and I will be their God: for they shall return unto me with their whole heart.* (Jer 24:7)

> *But let him that glorieth glory in this, that he understandeth and knoweth me, that I am the LORD which exercise lovingkindness, judgment, and righteousness, in the earth: for in these things I delight, saith the LORD.* (Jer 9:24)

> *Behold, we count them happy which endure. Ye have heard of the patience of Job, and have seen the end of the Lord; that the Lord is very pitiful, and of tender mercy.* (Jas 5:11)

> *This then is the message which we have heard of him, and declare unto you, that God is light, and in him is no darkness at all.* (1 Jn 1:5)

God is personal and of upright character. He cares about His children, offering us security and assurance of our future:

These things have I written unto you that believe on the name of the Son of God; that ye may know that ye have eternal life, and that ye may believe on the name of the Son of God. (1 Jn 5:13)

Unlike an impersonal force, or a capricious counterfeit deity, our all-powerful God knows the future, is involved in it, and brings about the outcomes He desires:

I'm telling you this now, before it happens, so that when it does happen, you may believe that I AM. (Jn 13:19 ISV)

Behold, I am the LORD, the God of all flesh: is there anything too hard for me? (Jer 32:27)

Declaring the end from the beginning, and from ancient times the things that are not yet done, saying, My counsel shall stand, and I will do all my pleasure... (Isa 46:10)

For I am the LORD: I will speak, and the word that I shall speak shall come to pass; it shall be no more prolonged: for in your days, O rebellious house, will I say the word, and will perform it, saith the Lord GOD. (Ezek 12:25)

The God of the Bible is unique because He has always existed. He declares that He is the only God:

Unto thee it was shewed, that thou mightest know that the LORD he is God; there is none else beside him. (Deut 4:35)

Before the mountains were brought forth, or ever thou hadst formed the earth and the world, even from everlasting to everlasting, thou art God. (Ps 90:2)

Ye are my witnesses, saith the LORD, and my servant whom I have chosen: that ye may know and believe me, and understand that I am he: before me there was no God formed, neither shall there be after me. I, even I, am the LORD; and beside me there is no saviour. I have declared, and have saved, and I have shewed, when there was no strange god among you: therefore ye are my witnesses saith the LORD, that I am God. Yea, before the day was I am he; and there is none that can deliver out of my hand: I will work, and who shall let it? (Isa 43:10-13)

A force, lacking personhood, cannot give the world spiritual concepts such as beauty, liberty, or love. The competing gods of the false religions cannot prove themselves to be the one true God. The God of the Bible is the one and only Creator:

Thus saith the LORD, thy redeemer, and he that formed thee from the womb, I am the LORD that maketh all things; that stretcheth forth the heavens alone; that spreadeth abroad the earth by myself... (Isa 44:24)

*I have made the earth, and created man upon it: I, even my
hands, have stretched out the heavens, and all their host have I
commanded.* (Isa 45:12)

*For thus saith the LORD that created the heavens; God himself
that formed the earth and made it; he hath established it, he
created it not in vain, he formed it to be inhabited: I am the
LORD; and* there is *none else.* (Isa 45:18)

Because of the multitude of false religions, the objections to who
God is can be complex, so a simple response to this objection may be
preferable. Asking the hearer if he is willing to explain his disbelief in
the biblical God may reveal that he has no concrete reason for denying
who God is. If he does have a reason, another simple question may
suffice, such as asking him what evidence he has of his conviction.
He may have faulty "evidence" or none at all, and allowing him to
realize this for himself may be more effective than trying to convince
him. A question such as, "Are you absolutely certain about your
eternal destiny?" can be much more powerful than any argument or
explanation. Strange ideas are endless, but God offers proof of who He
is, therefore providing security and peace to those who believe, and
evidence to those who are willing to hear the testimony of His word.

Considering who God is, one of the most wonderful things about Him
is that He lets us know that He understands us. He isn't looking to
pounce every time we fail. He knows we are frail, and weak, and that
we need His tender mercy:

The LORD is merciful and gracious, slow to anger, and plenteous in mercy. He will not always chide: neither will he keep his anger for ever. He hath not dealt with us after our sins; nor rewarded us according to our iniquities. For as the heaven is high above the earth, so great is his mercy toward them that fear him. As far as the east is from the west, so far hath he removed our transgressions from us. Like as a father pitieth his children, so the LORD pitieth them that fear him. For he knoweth our frame; he remembereth that we are dust. (Ps 103:8-14)

Unlike the elements of the earth, or some kind of "force," or a distant, unknowable god, our God saves. No religion in the world or in history can say the same. In every way He is a good God, an important truth to convey to those who are willing to hear who He really is.

CHAPTER 4

WHAT HE DID

Death, Burial, and Resurrection for Sin

Not by works of righteousness which we have done,
but according to his mercy he saved us... (Titus 3:5a)

Jesus Christ died on a cross as a sacrifice for sins. Among the various objections to what He did, the most common by far is the idea that His sacrifice is not sufficient to save. An insufficient sin payment requires that law-keeping or good works be added to the work of Christ, a belief commonly referred to as "legalism." Such objections are closely related to the topic of Chapter 6, which addresses faith alone for salvation. Whether an objector to "what He did" mixes law with grace, or denies that it even happened, his disbelief in the death, burial and resurrection of Jesus Christ as a completed payment for sin is a rejection of the Gospel of Christ, found in 1 Corinthians 15:1-4.

It Didn't Happen?

The Bible contains the detailed historical record of the death, burial and resurrection of Jesus Christ, including the fact that there were hundreds of witnesses to the event. Although Christians know that the resurrection is a documented event of ancient history, deniers exist. For example, a Muslim or a Jew may deny the resurrection of Jesus because both Islam and modern, non-biblical Judaism dispute the historical record. In the first case, Islam teaches that Jesus was not crucified:

"That they said (in boast), 'We killed Christ Jesus the son
of Mary, the Messenger of Allah'; - but they killed him not,
nor crucified him, but so it was made to appear to them, and
those who differ therein are full of doubts, with no (certain)
knowledge, but only conjecture to follow, for of a surety they
killed him not." (Koran, Sura 4:157)

Similarly, Judaism denies the resurrection of Christ and does not
accept Him as its prophesied savior. The Bible testifies that in an effort
to cover up His resurrection, the chief priests and elders of Israel
bribed the Roman guards to lie about the disappearance of Jesus' body:

And when they were assembled with the elders, and had taken
counsel, they gave large money unto the soldiers, Saying, Say ye,
His disciples came by night, and stole him away while we slept.
And if this come to the governor's ears, we will persuade him, and
secure you. So they took the money, and did as they were taught:
and this saying is commonly reported among the Jews until this
day. (Mt 28:12-15)

It Happened, But...

Even those who assent to the biblical record of history and its testimony
of Jesus' sacrifice may object to the sufficiency of Jesus' payment for
sin. Some objections are easily-detected lists of "do's" to get saved and
"don'ts" to avoid the lake of fire. Others are more subtle, manifesting
themselves in doubts about the surety of forgiveness or of faith alone to
receive it. Learning that someone believes that works are necessary for
salvation, or that morality is what makes someone a Christian, could

be that uncomfortable moment when you realize that the person next to you in the church pew is the one who needs to hear the Gospel.

The belief that something needs to be added to the death, burial and resurrection of Jesus Christ for sin is a rejection of Him as a satisfactory sacrifice. Here are some variations of denying the sufficiency of the cross:

"You have to be good." Some sins are so bad or some people are so evil that they are disqualified from heaven, but most people are not, and will get to heaven. Believing that man can be good, this objector denies the inherent sinfulness of man and nullifies Christ's payment for the sins of the world, replacing it with human morality.

"I need faith and..." Believing alone is not sufficient to receive the payment for sin; we must do something also. Salvation amounts to a partnership between Jesus and me as co-redeemers, in which we both contribute something to salvation. This is often a plainly-stated denial, such as a belief in the necessity of a church ritual.

"Some of the Law is still in effect." Certain works must be done or laws obeyed to qualify for heaven. The practical object of faith is the works or laws. A common example is believing that it is possible to keep the 10 commandments.

These are all forms of legalism, also called law-keeping, law-works, or works salvation. Legalism is a misunderstanding or denial of the gracious nature of salvation, and its variations are merely differences in what is emphasized. Whether some activity must be avoided or some merit added in order to gain salvation, legalism is a rejection of the Gospel of Christ. Determining the particular nature of the objection will help in your response. An easy example to use when trying to determine if a person believes in the sufficiency of Christ's sacrifice for sin is the universally agreed upon most-evil-person-ever.

"So you think anyone can go to heaven? Even Hitler?!"

For there is no respect of persons with God. (Ro 2:11)

Comparison is at the heart of human achievement; we evaluate our efforts by comparing them to others. But salvation is not an achievement; it is a gracious gift. We gain something that we do not deserve, simply by faith in what someone else accomplished on our behalf. Faith is the perfect way to access grace, because it excludes any kind of human effort. Mighty or weak, genius or average, pious or fallen, we are all able to receive forgiveness of sins...even Hitler. It may seem unfair that an evil person has the same opportunity for salvation as a sweet grandmother, but if fairness was the standard, we would all be in the lake of fire. Our unworthiness for heaven is not in comparison to others, but in comparison to the perfect holiness of God. God has no "respect of persons," meaning He deals with all men justly, and without bias, even including Hitler (Ro 2:11, Acts 10:34, Eph 6:9, Col 3:25).

Some hearers think too well of humanity (excepting Hitler) and misunderstand human nature. A common refrain is, "People are basically good." This contradicts the biblical declaration that we are all born sinners, in need of salvation from sin, and in possession of nothing worthy of God. Children are a familiar example of this; they do not need to be taught to hit their siblings, hoard their toys, or say, "No!" to Mommy. The assessment of our condition as sinners is not from our point of view, but from the perfect and holy perspective of our Creator, as expressed by King David:

Behold, I was shapen in iniquity; and in sin did my mother conceive me. (Ps 51:5)

Those who trust in their good works think that they have something of value to offer God. But God excludes human effort for salvation, proclaiming that even our "righteousnesses," our very *best* works, are filthy and tainted with sin:

But we are all as an unclean thing, *and all our righteousnesses* are *as filthy rags; and we all do fade as a leaf; and our iniquities, like the wind, have taken us away.* (Isaiah 64:6)

Upon understanding God's evaluation of our human efforts, we dare not offer Him the dirty rags of our works, but can only fall before Him in need of His mercy to save us. If one believes that all of us "good people" are qualified for heaven, while Hitler and a few others are not, then human merit is a factor in salvation. Such a view can only render the death, burial and resurrection of Jesus Christ insufficient to save. Making no meritorious distinctions among men, God's word declares that Jesus Christ died for the sins of the whole world:

*And he is the propitiation for our sins: and not for ours only, but also **for the** sins of **the whole world**.* (1 Jn 2:2, emphasis added)

*For God so loved the world, that he gave his only begotten Son, that whosoever believeth in him should not perish, but have everlasting life. For God sent not his Son into the world to condemn the world; but **that the world through him might be saved**.* (Jn 3:16-17 emphasis added)

*And said unto the woman, Now we believe, not because of thy saying: for we have heard him ourselves, and know that this is indeed the Christ, **the Saviour of the world**.* (Jn 4:42 emphasis added)

*I am the living bread which came down from heaven: if any man eat of this bread, he shall live for ever: and the bread that I will give is my flesh, which **I will give for the life of the world**.* (Jn 6:51 emphasis added)

*To wit, that God was in Christ, **reconciling the world** unto himself, not imputing their trespasses unto them; and hath committed unto us the word of reconciliation.* (2 Cor 5:19 emphasis added)

Because many will reject the payment for their sins, the whole world will not be in heaven. But, all those who believed the Gospel of Christ for salvation will be there.

"Yes, I believe the gospel, but I still need to do my share."

And whosoever liveth and believeth in me shall never die. Believest thou this? (Jn 11:26)

Some who object to what Jesus did, do so indirectly. Such an objector might agree that there is a universal need for salvation, that mankind is sinful and that God is just in requiring a penalty for sin. Even so, misunderstanding that Christians are called to do good works *after* salvation is what leads him away from the sufficiency of the cross. Because God allows Christians to share in His work here on earth, this objector sees no rejection of grace in "doing his part" in salvation as well. The partnership between God and His ministers and teachers is misapplied, and is, therefore, thought to help secure salvation. Our partnership with God, however, is only after we are cleansed by the blood of Christ.

Although it is unlikely that anyone would consider himself a co-redeemer, this is the unavoidable conclusion if one must contribute to one's own salvation. The objector who cannot believe that there is nothing we can do to be saved can be shown the testimony of scripture. In many places it teaches that we are to simply believe in order to receive this gift:

To him give all the prophets witness, that through his name whosoever believeth in him shall receive remission of sins. (Acts 10:43)

For the wages of sin is death; but the gift of God is eternal life through Jesus Christ our Lord. (Ro 6:23)

*But God, who is rich in mercy, for his great love wherewith he loved us, Even when we were dead in sins, hath quickened us together with Christ, (by grace ye are saved;) And hath raised us up together, and made us sit together in heavenly places in Christ Jesus: That in the ages to come he might shew the exceeding riches of his grace in his kindness toward us through Christ Jesus. For by grace are ye saved through faith; and that not of yourselves: it is the **gift** of God: **Not of works**, lest any man should boast.*
(Eph 2:4-9, emphasis added)

"So you just throw out part of the Bible? I believe all of it!"

For whatsoever things were written aforetime were written for our learning, that we through patience and comfort of the scriptures might have hope. (Ro 15:4)

Many objections to the death, burial and resurrection of Jesus Christ for sin are made because the objector does not believe that His sacrifice can save without the addition of something else. Often what is added is Old Testament law. This objector believes the Bible, and therefore thinks that all of it is currently applicable. He is not aware that God administered the Nation of Israel by law, but administers the church by the principle of grace. Failing to make a distinction between the Old and New Testaments is a common source of legalism.

Numerous Bible verses specifically exclude law-works both for initial salvation and for Christian living. Adherence to a works or law system is a rejection of the gracious gift of salvation. God is not impressed with our works; He is impressed with the work of the Son. Anyone who rejects the payment of Jesus Christ for his sins will spend eternity in the lake of fire, paying for his own sins (Rev 20:14-15).

If law-works are needed for salvation, then Jesus' sacrificial death did not fully pay for sin. But we know that His payment was sufficient and accepted by God. After Jesus died, He descended into "the lower parts of the earth" (Eph 4:9, 1 Pet 3:19). He did not remain there, however, but returned from the dead. The debt owed on every sin had already been paid on the cross. That is why Jesus proclaimed, "It is finished" (Jn 19:30).

Whom God hath raised up, having loosed the pains of death: because it was not possible that he should be holden of it. (Acts 2:24)

He seeing this before spake of the resurrection of Christ, that his soul was not left in hell, neither his flesh did see corruption. (Acts 2:31)

A relatable example of a payment made in full is that when I have paid off my car loan, that debt is gone. If Jesus pays my sin debt, it's gone too. But, if I am doing works to please, appease, or pay God, I am in fact offering those works as a payment for my sins, instead of accepting the free gift of salvation. It cannot be both. Either something is a free gift, or it is worked for and earned or purchased. Any payment makes an item received no longer a gift. Believing that the salvation purchased by Christ must be gained or earned by the sinner means that either the gift has been rejected, or the offer has not been understood.

No Defense for Law

The charge that Christians have thrown out the Old Testament is serious and deserves additional attention. It is not a rejection of the Old Testament to believe that Jesus' death paid for all sin without the works of the Law. The Old Testament Law and prophets made obvious man's need for a savior, and identified Him when He arrived. Testifying to the love, faithfulness, and longsuffering of God as He dealt with His chosen nation, Israel, the Old Testament is instructive and comforting to Christians (Ro 15:4).

Efforts to be obedient to law are exceedingly common among many who call themselves Christians. Law-keeping can take as many forms as people have ideas for trying to impress God. Some are personal, while others are denominational, attached to a certain type of church. Some are unique, and others are variations of Old Testament Law. Trying to incorporate Old Testament Law into the grace system of the church is the most widely used form of law-works, and is our focus here.

There are several reasons why Old Testament law-keeping cannot be part of salvation. Firstly, it is a denial of the sufficiency of Christ's sacrifice for sin, and secondly it is impossible for any man to keep even a fraction of it. The Law had 613 requirements; nobody can even keep the most well-known 10. The same would be true for any law system; no matter what rules a person sets for himself, eventually he will break them.

The Old Testament Law of Moses, or Mosaic Law, expressed God's *perfect* standard. Therefore, any lesser level of performance in an effort to gain salvation has already fallen short. No person other than Jesus

Christ has ever perfectly kept the Law, so if it is needed for entrance into heaven, nobody is getting in.

For neither they themselves who are circumcised keep the law; but desire to have you circumcised, that they may glory in your flesh.
(Gal 6:13)

Now therefore why tempt ye God, to put a yoke upon the neck of the disciples, which neither our fathers nor we were able to bear?
(Acts 15:10)

A third problem with attaching the Law to salvation is that the Law was never intended to save. Its purpose was to reveal sin, and to show those who lived under it their need for a savior. Laws of any kind do nothing more than inform a lawbreaker of his violation; they cannot deliver the lawbreaker from its penalty. For example, if I drive past a 35 mph speed limit sign while driving 55, it shows me that I am guilty. Obeying the law in the future does not change the fact that I broke it in the past, nor exonerate me from the consequences.

*But now **we are delivered from the law**, that being dead wherein we were held; that we should serve in newness of spirit, and not in the oldness of the letter. What shall we say then? Is the law sin? God forbid. Nay, **I had not known sin, but by the law:** for I had not known lust, except the law had said, Thou shalt not covet.*
(Ro 7:6-7, emphasis added)

*For **the law made nothing perfect,** but the bringing in of a better hope did; by the which we draw nigh unto God.* (Heb 7:19, emphasis added)

*For **the law** having a shadow of good things to come, and not the very image of the things, **can never with those sacrifices** which they offered year by year continually **make the comers thereunto perfect.*** (Heb 10:1, emphasis added)

*Wherefore the law was our schoolmaster to bring us unto Christ, that we might be justified by faith. But **after that faith is come, we are no longer under a schoolmaster.*** (Gal 3:24-25, emphasis added)

*For **what the law could not do,** in that it was weak through the flesh, God sending his own Son in the likeness of sinful flesh, and for sin, condemned sin in the flesh...* (Ro 8:3, emphasis added)

For those who have the righteousness of Christ, the Law serves no purpose. Powerless to remedy or undo the fact that it has been violated, it is only a revealer of sin, and not a solution to it. Only by God's grace can sin be forgiven. Law, in fact, "frustrates" grace, making Christ's victory over sin of no effect:

I do not frustrate the grace of God: for if righteousness come by the law, then Christ is dead in vain. (Gal 2:21)

For I through the law am dead to the law, that I might live unto God. (Gal 2:19)

The reason that law frustrates grace is because one must reject gracious salvation in order to instead work to earn it. Law also frustrates grace because the sin nature is enticed by it; that which law denies becomes desirable:

> *The sting of death is sin; and the strength of sin is the law.*
> (1 Cor 15:56)

The practice of law-works is the opposite of accepting God's grace by faith. They are wholly incompatible:

> *And if by grace, then is it no more of works: otherwise grace is no more grace. But if it be of works, then is it no more grace: otherwise work is no more work.* (Ro 11:6)

> *Where is boasting then? It is excluded. By what law? of works? Nay: but by the law of faith. Therefore we conclude that a man is justified by faith without the deeds of the law.* (Ro 3:27-28)

> *For if Abraham were justified by works, he hath whereof to glory; but not before God. For what saith the scripture? Abraham believed God, and it was counted unto him for righteousness. Now to him that worketh is the reward not reckoned of grace, but of debt. But to him that worketh not, but believeth on him that justifieth the ungodly, his faith is counted for righteousness. Even as David also describeth the blessedness of the man, unto whom God imputeth righteousness without works, Saying, Blessed are they whose iniquities are forgiven, and whose sins are covered. Blessed is the man to whom the Lord will not impute sin.* (Ro 4:2-8)

Nevertheless knowing that a man is not justified by the works of the Law but through faith in Christ Jesus, even we have believed in Christ Jesus, so that we may be justified by faith in Christ and not by the works of the Law; since by the works of the Law no flesh will be justified. (Gal 2:16)

The justification of the believer before God is by faith in Jesus Christ, not by works. The testimony of scripture is also clear that the administration of the church is by grace, not by the Mosaic Law:

For sin shall not have dominion over you: for ye are not under the law, but under grace. (Ro 6:14)

But if ye be led of the Spirit, ye are not under the law. (Gal 5:18)

Be not thou therefore ashamed of the testimony of our Lord, nor of me his prisoner: but be thou partaker of the afflictions of the gospel according to the power of God; Who hath saved us, and called us with an holy calling, not according to our works, but according to his own purpose and grace, which was given us in Christ Jesus before the world began, But is now made manifest by the appearing of our Saviour Jesus Christ, who hath abolished death, and hath brought life and immortality to light through the gospel... (2 Tim 1:8-10)

Adding to the hopelessness of law-keeping is that Old Testament legalists cannot honestly claim to keep the Law, which included temple sacrifices and stonings, for example. They can only select parts of Israel's law to follow. But the Law is one entity, a complete and indivisible package, representing God's holiness. Breaking any part of it breaks His entire Law, and performing only part of it does not qualify as keeping the Law. Trying to keep some fragment of the Law is a futile religious exercise.

For whosoever shall keep the whole law, and yet offend in one point, he is guilty of all. (Jas 2:10)

For as many as are of the works of the law are under the curse: for it is written Cursed is every one that continueth not in all things which are written in the book of the law to do them. But that no man is justified by the law in the sight of God, it is evident: for, The just shall live by faith. And the law is not of faith: but, The man that doeth them shall live in them. Christ hath redeemed us from the curse of the law, being made a curse for us: for it is written, Cursed is every one that hangeth on a tree... (Gal 3:10-13)

For I testify again to every man that is circumcised, that he is a debtor to do the whole law. Christ is become of no effect unto you, whosoever of you are justified by the law; ye are fallen from grace. (Gal 5:3-4)

For Christ is the end of the law for righteousness to every one that believeth. For Moses describeth the righteousness which is of the law, That the man which doeth those things shall live by them. (Ro 10:4-5)

Christians are not throwing out the Old Testament by not keeping the Law. We recognize that the Law had its role, as did the Garden of Eden, Noah's ark, Solomon's temple, and many other things that are not part of God's current program. We see the Law for what it was and walk by grace through faith, a vastly superior program given to administer the body of Christ (Heb 7:19, 7:22, 8:6).

"I do my best and try to be a good person. I've lived a pretty good life, never cheated on my wife, or used drugs, or killed anyone. I sure don't live like so-and-so. I don't think I'm that bad that I deserve to burn in hell!"

Some who object to what Jesus did seem to have little awareness of their sinfulness. Such a person knows of people "worse" than he is, and therefore, the death, burial and resurrection of Jesus Christ for sins is irrelevant. He has a law of his own which goes something like this: "Whatever I do is good enough by my own standard." God's evaluation of his life might be helpful to this objector. It is God's standard, not ours, that will determine our eternal destiny, and judgment day is coming. The scripture is clear, both about mankind's lack of righteousness, and about the destination of those who refuse the righteousness offered by Christ:

> *What then? are we better than they? No, in no wise: for we have before proved both Jews and Gentiles, that they are all under sin; As it is written, There is none righteous, no, not one: There is none that understandeth, there is none that seeketh after God. They are all gone out of the way, they are together become unprofitable; there is none that doeth good, no, not one. Their throat is an open*

sepulchre; with their tongues they have used deceit; the poison of asps is under their lips: Whose mouth is full of cursing and bitterness: Their feet are swift to shed blood: Destruction and misery are in their ways: And the way of peace have they not known: There is no fear of God before their eyes. Now we know that what things soever the law saith, it saith to them who are under the law: that every mouth may be stopped, and all the world may become guilty before God. Therefore by the deeds of the law there shall no flesh be justified in his sight: for by the law is the knowledge of sin. But now the righteousness of God without the law is manifested, being witnessed by the law and the prophets; Even the righteousness of God which is by faith of Jesus Christ unto all and upon all them that believe: for there is no difference: For all have sinned, and come short of the glory of God; Being justified freely by his grace through the redemption that is in Christ Jesus: Whom God hath set forth to be a propitiation through faith in his blood, to declare his righteousness for the remission of sins that are past, through the forbearance of God; To declare, I say, at this time his righteousness: that he might be just, and the justifier of him which believeth in Jesus. (Ro 3:9-26; see also Ps 14:1-3, 53:1-3)

And I saw the dead, small and great, stand before God; and the books were opened: and another book was opened, which is the book of life: and the dead were judged out of those things which were written in the books, according to their works. And the sea gave up the dead which were in it; and death and hell delivered up the dead which were in them: and they were judged every man according to their works. And death and hell were cast into the lake of fire. This is the second death. And whosoever was not found written in the book of life was cast into the lake of fire. (Rev 20:12-15)

God hates sin, and heaven would not be heavenly with sinners in it, so every sin must be sent away. Only with the righteousness of Jesus Christ can we enter into the presence of the Father (Jn 16:8-11). A person who believes in his own goodness, or who thinks he only needs to be better than somebody else, may not be open to the Gospel until he recognizes his own sinfulness before God. Sometimes asking him questions about his foibles and failings can trigger some awareness. Whether or not he believes the testimony of scripture regarding his condition may depend upon his level of respect for the Bible. This objector must accept that only by faith in Jesus' death, burial and resurrection for sin can one attain His righteousness and enter heaven.

"I've been a Christian my whole life. I was born in a Christian home, I was baptized and confirmed, I go to church, pray, and have even read the whole Bible. I am offended that you would bring up salvation!"

For Christ sent me not to baptize, but to preach the gospel: not with wisdom of words, lest the cross of Christ should be made of none effect. (1 Cor 1:17)

An objection which comes from a church attendee may be the most difficult to overcome. Such an objector may proclaim grace, but in practice he is legalistic, adding works to the Gospel. Legalism can be strict, structured law-keeping, but it can also be soft, personalized "do-good-ism," which not only seems harmless, but is altruistic, even sacrificial. This person does not see that he follows a law of his own making, a set of standards by which he measures "Christianity." Such a system may include religious acts such as water baptism, confirmation or church attendance. It may be some version of "comparing themselves among themselves," considering himself a Christian because his lifestyle choices are superior to the choices of others (2 Cor 10:12). He may also view Christianity to be something one is born into, like being born into an Irish family. For him, the death, burial and resurrection of Christ is almost a non-issue because Christianity is his lifestyle. He is "living the Christian life," ...except without the life part.

"Lifestyle Christianity" aka The Good People

Because of the prevalence of the view of Christianity as a lifestyle, it deserves further attention. Many people define Christianity in the same way as does the world at large; it comes through cultural affiliation, the receiving of sacraments, or some other external means. Viewing the Christian faith as a moral lifestyle choice is an indirect objection to what Jesus did, because His work is not the object of faith. This objector may be aware that he does not even meet his own standard of morality, but he is doing a better job than the next guy, whose standard is lower. His reasoning does not take into account that the standard for heaven is God's perfect holiness, which cannot be achieved by lifestyle choices, however upstanding they may be.

Christianity is a spiritual birth, not a lifestyle. It is not passed on through a family. It is not conferred through baptism or any other church activity. Without spiritual regeneration, we are merely trying to live our best in our sinful flesh, and we cannot enter into a relationship with God. When sharing the Gospel with a hearer who is stuck on the idea that he is living a Christian lifestyle, you may need to distinguish external moral living from the new birth, which is explained in Chapter 1. Spiritual regeneration, not good living, is what makes us Christians and is accessed by believing the message of 1 Corinthians 15:1-4, the Gospel of Christ, and by no other means.

"What about all the good things I have done? I think I have done more good than evil. In the end, I think my good deeds will outweigh my bad deeds."

Not by works of righteousness which we have done, but according to his mercy he saved us, by the washing of regeneration, and renewing of the Holy Ghost... (Titus 3:5)

Balancing Act

A classic version of works for salvation is the good old scale of balance, which compares my good works to my bad works, instead of comparing all my works to those of Christ on the cross. Characterizing God's judgment as a scale or balance, like a statue of Lady Justice in a courtroom, has an inherent problem, however. Lady Justice is not comparing good deeds to bad deeds; she is weighing evidence! Is there evidence that I am a sinner? Yes, indeed; we all are. As with every legalistic thinker, the objector who weighs good against bad has set his own standard, and in this case has determined that he has done less harm than good.

The Bible contains nothing to support the idea that one can do a certain number of "bad deeds" as long as a greater amount of good is done. If it did, how would "bad" be measured? What qualifies as bad? How much "good" needs to be done for each bad deed? Since the Bible's judgment has already been excluded, whose estimation of good is used? The problem with this view quickly becomes apparent upon scrutiny.

Far from accepting a certain amount of sin, God, the perfect judge, is holy and is offended by all sin. Only a corrupt judge would exonerate a man for murder because he once saved someone's life. To think that Almighty God would implement such a system is not reasonable, because a system that balances good deeds against bad is allowing those bad deeds and deeming them permissible, as long as they are "balanced with good."

On the practical side, how many "good deeds" does a person ever really do? Most things people do are out of necessity and self-interest. Meeting obligations, obeying laws, and fulfilling agreements can hardly be characterized as "good deeds." Some religions count every prayer as a good deed, but for what do most people pray? Are most of the world's prayers for wants and wishes? How many plead as David did to do nothing but the will of God (Ps 143:10)? The person who is relying upon an accumulation of good deeds is trusting in his own achievements rather than in the death, burial and resurrection of Jesus Christ for the sins of the world. For salvation, each person must be convinced that the Gospel of Christ, found in 1 Corinthians 15:1-4, is true and, therefore, sufficient to save.

"I don't agree with you; I have my own beliefs."
*"I sincerely believe in my faith, and I think God will
honor that."*

Sanctify them through thy truth: thy word is truth. (Jn 17:17)

Yet another way to object to the value of what Jesus did is to deny the
unique nature of His ministry to humanity. This objector counts any
religious belief valid, and, therefore, whatever form that belief takes
becomes a personal works system. He assumes that God will bow to
whatever religion he wishes to practice. Putting himself in God's place,
he makes God submissive to his idea or plan. In this view, the sacrifice
of Jesus for sin is of no greater value than any fanciful religious notion.

Wishful Thinking

For the person who has his own unique beliefs, or feels comfortable in
the religion of his choice, "sincerity" is often used as the standard and
the measure of faith. It is truth, however, and not sincerity that matters
to God. What evidence does the objector have that what he believes
is true? Is there evidence that God honors false religion if it practiced
with sincerity? The Bible claims to contain the truth; therefore its
author cannot approve of competing and contradictory faith claims.
If the hearer has little respect for or belief in the Bible, he may refuse
to consider scripture references. But as ministers of the Gospel, we can
attempt to offer information and answer questions, allowing the Spirit
of God to do His convincing work as to the truth of scripture:

*Jesus saith unto him, I am the way, the truth, and the life: no man
cometh unto the Father, but by me.* (Jn 14:6)

And ye shall know the truth, and the truth shall make you free.
(Jn 8:32)

*And this is life eternal, that they might know thee the only true
God, and Jesus Christ, whom thou hast sent.* (Jn 17:3)

*And for their sakes I sanctify myself, that they also might be
sanctified through the truth.* (Jn 17:19)

In whom ye also trusted, *after that ye heard the word of truth, the
gospel of your salvation: in whom also after that ye believed, ye
were sealed with that holy Spirit of promise.* (Eph 1:13)

*For the hope which is laid up for you in heaven, whereof ye heard
before in the word of the truth of the gospel.* (Col 1:5)

*For this cause also thank we God without ceasing, because, when
ye received the word of God which ye heard of us, ye received* it
*not as the word of men, but as it is in truth, the word of God,
which effectually worketh also in you that believe.* (1 Thess 2:13)

*But we are bound to give thanks alway to God for you, brethren
beloved of the Lord, because God hath from the beginning chosen
you to salvation through sanctification of the Spirit and belief of
the truth...* (2 Thess 2:13)

*Who will have all men to be saved, and to come unto the
knowledge of the truth.* (1 Tim 2:4)

But if I tarry long, that thou mayest know how thou oughtest to behave thyself in the house of God, which is the church of the living God, the pillar and ground of the truth. (1 Tim 3:15)

To see the truth means to see things as they really are. Only God can see the truth of all things, therefore we need His word to teach us what is true. A person can be sincere and yet be wrong. Therefore, regardless of one's sincerity in believing a lie, in regard to eternity, only that which is true is of value. The world is full of facts, but the Bible, God's word to mankind, is truth.

Many hearers of the Gospel of Christ will object to what Jesus did. They might insist that more must be done, denying that faith in Christ's finished work is sufficient to save. Others will define Christianity as merely moral living, disregarding what Jesus did altogether. To meet some moral lifestyle standard, an adherent to this belief will need to follow a "do's" and "don'ts" system, rather than accepting Jesus' payment for sins on the cross by faith. Including some behaviors and excluding others for the purpose of salvation is a form of legalism, an external system of rules. Christianity specifically excludes itself as a law system, proclaiming that God's law had a purpose which has since been fulfilled (Gal 3:24-25). Christianity is a spiritual birth: an internal change by grace through faith. A godly lifestyle is the outworking of that internal change, not its cause (Phil 2:12). The issue of legalism is vast and complex. As with every objection to the Gospel, a Christian's best tool is a thorough understanding of the Gospel by which we are saved, found in 1 Corinthians 15:1-4.

CHAPTER 5

WHY I NEED IT

For Sin

It is a fearful thing to fall into the hands of the living God.

(Heb 10:31)

Objections to the Gospel of Christ are commonly about specific doctrines such as the deity of Christ, the sufficiency of grace, or the inerrancy of the Bible. Another type of objection may be more challenging to a Christian witness because it is not necessarily about a particular teaching. Rather than taking issue with the particulars of Christianity, some hearers are disinterested, lacking concern about eternity and salvation. They may find matters of faith to be foolish or a waste of time. Some believe they are already "good with God," while others are not concerned because they do not believe in the afterlife. They are in denial regarding their sinful state and their accountability to their Creator. Wanting to follow their own way, they reject their need for a solution to sin.

"What is someone dying on a cross going to do for me? Religion is for other people, and a crutch for the weak. I don't need saving."

He has fixed a day in which He will judge the world in righteousness through a Man whom He has appointed, having furnished proof to all men by raising Him from the dead.

(Acts 17:31 NASB)

Going to jail or prison used to be referred to as "paying a debt to society." The phrase recognizes that when someone commits a crime, he has harmed his community or a member of it. Since the criminal cannot undo what has been done, he must pay for his crime in some way, such as with a fine, imprisonment, or even with his life. Committing a sin also creates a debt, but with God:

"Against thee, thee only, have I sinned..." (Ps 51:4a).

Even a person who does not acknowledge wronging God is unlikely to claim to have never done anything wrong. Each of us has a God-given conscience, and the knowledge exists that our lives and actions matter. Therefore, the real reason for objecting to the Gospel may not be due to disbelieving in sin, but in not wanting to be held accountable for it. Man is a sinner by nature, and sin's hallmark is rebellion against God. God's assessment of mankind can be helpful in breaking down a hearer's denial of the need for a solution to sin. The Bible tells us that we are born in sin, and that there is a consequence for sin:

Behold, I was shapen in iniquity; and in sin did my mother conceive me. (Ps 51:5)

But we are all as an unclean thing, and all our righteousnesses are as filthy rags; and we all do fade as a leaf; and our iniquities, like the wind, have taken us away. (Isa 64:6)

And Jesus said unto him, Why callest thou me good? there is none good but one, that is, God. (Mk 10:18; see also Mt 19:17; Lk 18:19)

For the wages of sin is death; but the gift of God is eternal life through Jesus Christ our Lord. (Ro 6:23)

Therefore thou art inexcusable, O man, whosoever thou art that judgest: for wherein thou judgest another, thou condemnest thyself; for thou that judgest doest the same things. But we are sure that the judgment of God is according to truth against them which commit such things. And thinkest thou this, O man, that judgest them which do such things, and doest the same, that thou shalt escape the judgment of God? Or despisest thou the riches of his goodness and forbearance and longsuffering; not knowing that the goodness of God leadeth thee to repentance? But after thy hardness and impenitent heart treasurest up unto thyself wrath against the day of wrath and revelation of the righteous judgment of God; Who will render to every man according to his deeds: To them who by patient continuance in well doing seek for glory and honour and immortality, eternal life: But unto them that are contentious, and do not obey the truth, but obey unrighteousness, indignation and wrath, Tribulation and anguish, upon every soul of man that doeth evil, of the Jew first, and also of the Gentile; But glory, honour, and peace, to every man that worketh good, to the Jew first, and also to the Gentile: For there is no respect of persons with God. ...In the day when God shall judge the secrets of men by Jesus Christ according to my gospel. (Ro 2:1-11, 16)

Each of us is tainted by sin in all we desire, think, say, and do. God's conclusion regarding mankind's goodness is, "There is none that does good, there is not even one" (Ro 3:12b NASB). Any person who is not as good as God is not qualified for heaven, and nothing he produces is good enough either. Remaining in denial about one's accountability to his Creator is a stall but not a solution. One day every person will face God and be held to account for what he did and said:

> So then every one of us shall give account of himself to God. (Ro 14:12)

> Nothing in all creation is hidden from God's sight. Everything is uncovered and laid bare before the eyes of him to whom we must give account. (Heb 4:13 NIV)

Each person must decide for himself whether he believes the Gospel of Christ, the message revealing God's solution to the problem of sin. The hearer may insist that "religion" is not for him, but if he acknowledges that he has offended God, perhaps he will consider the Bible's warning that he needs Jesus Christ to pay for his sins. If not, he will be separated from God forever, paying for his own sins in the lake of fire:

> And the devil that deceived them was cast into the lake of fire and brimstone, where the beast and the false prophet are, and shall be tormented day and night for ever and ever. And I saw a great white throne, and him that sat on it, from whose face the earth and the heaven fled away; and there was found no place for them. And I saw the dead, small and great, stand before God; and the books were opened: and another book was opened, which is the book of life: and the dead were judged out of those things which were written in the books, according to their works. And the sea gave up the dead which were in it; and death and hell delivered

up the dead which were in them: and they were judged every
man according to their works. And death and hell were cast into
the lake of fire. This is the second death. And whosoever was not
found written in the book of life was cast into the lake of fire.
(Rev 20:10-15)

Avoiding the lake of fire seems like a good reason to consider salvation.
Jesus gave Himself as the object of God's wrath against sin, taking our
punishment and dying in our place. Upon believing the Gospel, the
sinner is credited with the payment for sin made by Jesus Christ on
his behalf. That payment satisfied both the justice and the love of God;
the sin debt is justly satisfied, and the sinner is lovingly released from
the debt.

What About the Cross?

Part of the objection to one's need for salvation may be a lack of
appreciation for what was accomplished on the cross. From the
perspective of such objectors, many people have died on a cross, so
Jesus' death is not special. This unique death, however, fulfilled many
biblical prophecies (Ps 22:1-18, 31:5, 34:20, 69:21; Is 50:6, 52:14, 53:1-
12; Zech 11:12-13, 12:10).

It is God who chose this method for the Savior's death. The Bible does
not explain why a cross was used, but perhaps the horrific nature of
this manner of death was intended to portray the seriousness of sin.
We are told that under the Law, dying on a tree displayed that the
person was cursed by God:

Christ hath redeemed us from the curse of the law, being made a curse for us: for it is written, Cursed is every one that hangeth on a tree... (Gal 3:13)

And if a man have committed a sin worthy of death, and he be to be put to death, and thou hang him on a tree: His body shall not remain all night upon the tree, but thou shalt in any wise bury him that day; (for he that is hanged is accursed of God;) that thy land be not defiled, which the LORD thy God giveth thee for an inheritance. (Deut 21:22-23)

Sin is a curse upon mankind, and the death of our Savior provided release from that curse for all who believe the Gospel of Christ. A person who denies any accountability for sin, or insists that faith is for the weak, may be using the objections as a defense or holding them as sincere beliefs. In any case, our calling as Christians is to proclaim that faith in Jesus' sacrifice provides the deliverance from sin that every person needs.

"I don't need deliverance. God made me this way. Why should I believe a religion that says that I am not okay?"

...be ye reconciled to God. (2 Cor 5:20b)

As a culture, our interest in religion increasingly comes more from a consumer's viewpoint than from a sinner's. "What will it do for me?" is the mantra of our day, and behaviors formerly considered sin have been embraced. One would think that the consumer mindset would welcome the vast benefits of salvation, but it is not so, because society has rejected the view of mankind as sinners. Couple this attitude with the issues of sexuality and gender which have been pushed to the forefront of social discussion, and we find people standing in judgment of God for His disagreement with their views. This breath-taking stance is often defended with claims that some sins are traits which existed from birth, an issue which matters no more than whether a person was born with any other preference. A person's preferences have no bearing whatsoever on the fact that God both expects and deserves to be believed and obeyed.

The real issue is not when our preferences develop, but that there is a difference between who we are and what we do. Regardless of what we do or don't do in terms of sin, who we are is described in one word: sinners. Each man's nature leads him to seek or deny his preferences, indulging or suppressing them to varying degrees, depending upon his willpower and convictions. Regardless of one's views of how we each came to be who we are, God still asks us to live according to His will, and does not give special exception to any group of people or category of behavior. Our own nature, preferences, will or desires provide no excuse before God. If we deny our need for salvation from sin, He allows us to follow sin to its ultimate consequence:

> *Because that which may be known of God is manifest in them;*
> *for God hath shewed it unto them. For the invisible things*
> *of him from the creation of the world are clearly seen, being*
> *understood by the things that are made, even his eternal power*
> *and Godhead; so that they are without excuse: Because that,*
> *when they knew God, they glorified him not as God, neither*

were thankful; but became vain in their imaginations, and
their foolish heart was darkened. And even as they did not
like to retain God in their knowledge, God gave them over to a
reprobate mind, to do those things which are not convenient;
Being filled with all unrighteousness, fornication, wickedness,
covetousness, maliciousness; full of envy, murder, debate, deceit,
malignity; whisperers, Backbiters, haters of God, despiteful, proud,
boasters, inventors of evil things, disobedient to parents, Without
understanding, covenantbreakers, without natural affection,
implacable, unmerciful: Who knowing the judgment of God, that
they which commit such things are worthy of death, not only do
the same, but have pleasure in them that do them. (Ro 1:19-21,
28-32)

A hearer may have many reasons for denying his need for salvation, but the bottom line is that he does not want it. Rejecting the Gospel is an avoidance of the real issue, which is sin. Christian witnesses need not be drawn into debates about the nature of sin tendencies. We are to share the Gospel, and if the hearer believes, he will learn that God does not approve of every whim and desire of mankind. The believer who yields to the power of grace can also experience freedom from the power of sin. A holy God has standards. A powerful God provides deliverance. A loving God proclaims that the needed solution to sin is free, and can be found in 1 Corinthians 15:1-4.

"I don't need Jesus to die for me. I am not a sinner."

For all have sinned and come short of the glory of God. (Ro 3:23)

This objection to the need for salvation begs the question, "What does this person think a sinner is?" A correct definition of sin may be all that is needed to answer this objection. Jesus died for the sins of the world because every human being is a sinner, having fallen short of the glory of God. We don't have to do much to fall short of glory! God is perfect, and is offended by sin; we are indebted to God for disobeying Him. Jesus paid the sin debt that we owe by taking the punishment for sin upon Himself on the cross.

A common misunderstanding of sin is that being a sinner means that a person is "really bad" or does horrifically evil deeds. Some divide wrongs into seemingly harmless categories such as "little white lies," but God does not. In Revelation we see that liars are headed for the lake of fire right along with murderers. The point is that for God, sin is sin. All sin separates us from Him because God is holy.

But the fearful, and unbelieving, and the abominable, and murderers, and whoremongers, and sorcerers, and idolaters, and all liars, shall have their part in the lake which burneth with fire and brimstone: which is the second death. (Rev 21:8)

These six things doth the LORD hate: yea, seven are an abomination unto him: A proud look, a lying tongue, and hands that shed innocent blood, An heart that deviseth wicked imaginations, feet that be swift in running to mischief, A false witness that speaketh lies, and he that soweth discord among brethren. (Prov 6:16-19)

... for whatsoever is not of faith is sin. (Ro 14:23b)

Adam and Eve in the garden of Eden are a good example of this principle. Adam's sin was the worst sin in the history of mankind, bringing humanity from perfection to a cursed world, from innocence to a knowledge of evil, and from bliss to pain. Eating a piece of off-limits fruit would not typically be considered a horrific act; it was acting independently from God which made it so. God cursed the entire earth for one sin, so comparing God's evaluation of sin to his own may lead this objector to reconsider his standard for what makes someone a sinner. Sin doesn't just mean evil; it can be anything that is not according to God's will. Helping hearers understand how God defines sin is part of helping them to see why they need salvation. We are either perfect, or we are sinners, and sinners need a savior.

"I'll worry about getting saved later, sometime before I die."

... now is the accepted time; behold, now is the day of salvation. (2 Cor 6:2b)

Another way of objecting to one's need for what Jesus did is procrastination. It is a flawed plan, since no person knows how much time he has on earth. A Christian witness can suggest to the one objecting that he may not have an opportunity to make a lucid decision on his deathbed, encouraging him to at least consider the Gospel now.

Even if the hearer is not open to believing it, if he listens to the details of 1 Corinthians 15:1-4 now, he will have more information when that day comes.

Yet you do not know what your life will be like tomorrow. You are just a vapor that appears for a little while and then vanishes away. (Jas 4:14 NASB)

Like as a father pitieth his children, so the LORD pitieth them that fear him. For he knoweth our frame; he remembereth that we are dust. As for man, his days are as grass: as a flower of the field, so he flourisheth. For the wind passeth over it, and it is gone; and the place thereof shall know it no more. (Ps 103:13-16)

"I'm already a Christian. I just don't believe _____."

Sanctify them through thy truth: thy word is truth. (Jn 17:17)

Sometimes an objector does not know he is an objector because he sees no incompatibility between being a Christian and rejecting some of Christianity's tenets. Excusing oneself from a particular doctrine could come from an unbeliever who needs to hear the Gospel, or from a believer who does not understand the significance of scriptural inerrancy. Perhaps, for example, the objector claims to be a Christian, but denies hell. A Christian witness could explain to him that hell is a penalty for sin, and that if there is no penalty, there is no need for a savior. Without the Savior, there is no Christianity, because the object of our faith is our Savior and what He did for us. Following his objection to its logical conclusion will expose the problem of excluding it from Christian belief. If he is a Christian, recognizing the incompatibility of his belief with the Gospel may result in an immediate change of mind.

If explaining the objectionable doctrine does not bring about an "aha moment," the issue becomes why this person does not believe the testimony of the Bible on this point. Of immediate importance to a Christian witness is whether the disputed doctrine is a component of the Gospel of Christ. If it is, or if you are not sure how much of the Gospel the objector believes, attempt to engage him in a discussion of the Gospel. While additional objections may arise during the conversation and can be addressed, of primary importance is that you provide as much information as possible about the way of salvation.

"I don't need Jesus. There is nothing after death, just lights out."

For when the Gentiles, which have not the law, do by nature the things contained in the law, these, having not the law, are a law unto themselves: Which shew the work of the law written in their hearts, their conscience also bearing witness, and their thoughts the mean while accusing or else excusing one another... (Ro 2:14-15)

Sometimes denying one's need of salvation is coupled with the atheistic view that man is only a material being and that there is nothing beyond this world. Such a view denies the source of all morality, and yet the person who holds it almost certainly raises his children with rules, feels badly when he hurts someone, and likes to see justice done when a wrong is committed. The existence of man's conscience informs us that we are more than material beings. Material cannot create the concepts of right and wrong, or any other spiritual concept, such as liberty, beauty, or happiness. Exposing the contradiction between denying the existence of spiritual life while living by its principles may cause this person to consider that there may be more to human existence than what we see.

Another problem with the notion of man as material only is that it makes life completely pointless. For example, if death is just "lights out," why should any person bother acting rightly? If there is no judgment at the end, maybe we should stop trying so hard for a "better world" and relax a little. Doing more of what we want might be a better option than trying to follow all the world's rules. We can do good all our lives, but in a generation or two most of us are forgotten anyway. In this world, most of our lives don't amount to much, and then we don't exist anymore.

But most people do not believe that we no longer exist after death, or that our lives and actions do not matter. We believe that how we raise our children, our faithfulness in marriage and our honesty at work all have greater meaning than just the earthly rewards for doing so. Perhaps this objector will follow up by saying that doing rightly makes the world more enjoyable while we are here. While this is so, it does not explain how it is that people everywhere share so much agreement on what constitutes good and bad. Could that be because these ideas have a common source? The Bible informs us that we all have a God-given conscience. It also says that faith is reasonable and disbelief is foolish, and that judgment day is coming. Not only does our conscience proclaim the existence of God; the creation displays it too. God's word has also been proven true by the resurrection of Jesus Christ:

He has fixed a day in which He will judge the world in righteousness through a Man whom He has appointed, having furnished proof to all men by raising Him from the dead. (Acts 17:31 NASB)

And that we may be delivered from unreasonable and wicked men: for all men have not faith. (2 Thess 3:2)

For what if some did not believe? Will their unbelief make the faithfulness of God without effect? Certainly not! Indeed, let God be true but every man a liar. (Ro 3:3-4a NKJV)

The fool hath said in his heart, There is no God. They are corrupt, they have done abominable works, there is none that doeth good. (Ps 14:1)

Because that which may be known of God is manifest in them; for God hath shewed it unto them. For the invisible things of him from the creation of the world are clearly seen, being understood by the things that are made, even his eternal power and Godhead; so that they are without excuse. (Ro 1:19-20)

What we do, what we think, and even what our motives are, does matter. Eternity matters more, and it is real. Our Christian calling is to testify to the truth of scripture to all who will listen, helping them to see their need for salvation. It is left to the conscience and will of each hearer to believe the Gospel of Christ, or not to.

"I don't need religion; I am close to God when I _____."
"I'm a very spiritual person."

There is a way which seemeth right unto a man, but the end thereof are the ways of death. (Prov 14:12)

Another objection to why we need the Gospel is a belief held by many, that they have their "own way" to be close to God. God, however, has already revealed the way in which we can be close to Him, and He will not defer to whatever way a person conceives. Because we are sinners who need salvation, a relationship with God is only through His Son, the Lord Jesus Christ, by faith in the Gospel message of 1 Corinthians 15:1-4.

Although many claim to have found their own way to God, God's actual way is not difficult to find. As is commonly known by Christians, but may not be known by the hearer, the death, burial and resurrection of Jesus Christ for sin is a well-documented event in ancient history, and the Bible has been the best-selling book for as long as there have been books to sell. Amazingly, although many Christians suffer, are persecuted, and have every reason to abandon Jesus, the world sees that the faith has not been extinguished. Suggest to a hearer that God's way may be worth hearing about and considering. Perhaps there is some value in looking at facts, rather than assuming that an idea we have in our own mind is acceptable to God.

A witnessing opportunity may or may not be the time to address the definition of spirituality, but it is not what most people probably think it is. To be spiritual means to emanate the character of God. His virtues are produced in the believer by the Holy Spirit, and are known as the fruit of the Spirit (Gal 5:22-23). Being spiritual is only possible when a person is born again.

If we assume there is a God, we can also safely assume that He has His own ideas about how things should be done. The Bible is a credible authority to learn about God and why we need Him. We can suggest to hearers that it may be worth learning about rather than dismissed, and help them see their need for God's one and only way of salvation.

"Christians are hypocrites. Why should I be held accountable for what I do, when that famous Christian did _____?!"

Come now, and let us reason together, saith the LORD: though your sins be as scarlet, they shall be as white as snow; though they be red like crimson, they shall be as wool. (Isaiah 1:18)

It is not uncommon for people to judge Christianity by the disobedience of a few. Christian witnesses who face this objection to why we need the Gospel can share several points with hearers who focus on the sins or hypocrisy of somebody else. Firstly, Christians are individuals, so claiming that all are hypocrites, for example, is simply not factual. Secondly, what some people do in disobedience to the faith is not the fault of God or the faith, and therefore not a reason to reject it. Thirdly, every person will one day face God with his sins, regardless of whether it appears as if he got away with something in the present time. Denying one's need of a remedy for sin does not remove anyone from God's final accounting for sin. When compared to the nonbelieving world, God's people are held to a much higher standard in our earthly lives:

> For whom the Lord loveth he chasteneth, and scourgeth every son whom he receiveth. If ye endure chastening, God dealeth with you as with sons; for what son is he whom the father chasteneth not? (Heb 12:6-7)

> What then? are we better than they? No, in no wise: for we have before proved both Jews and Gentiles, that they are all under sin; As it is written, There is none righteous, no, not one... (Ro 3:9-10)

The Bible is not a leaflet for a reason; everybody needs much instruction and has much to learn. There is not a person alive who lives in perfect accordance with his own values, much less God's, so anyone can be deemed a hypocrite. Encourage a hearer to look to his own failings, then offer him the solution; faith in the Gospel of Christ. Share with him that Christians are forgiven, but they have no license to sin. Some even face discipline from their Father for persistent sin, but on judgment day, they will not pay with their lives. Jesus already did.

"I can believe what I want."

Absolutely, yes you can! This objector may be assuming that you are going to argue the point or try to force your beliefs on him. You can instead delight him with the fact that you agree; he can indeed believe what he wants to. He may not, however, enjoy the result of entrusting his life to an idea which has no merit. This hearer may be willing to consider the importance of having some evidence of his eternal destiny.

He may also recognize that in any situation, there is a problem with believing things which are not true. Crossing one's fingers and hoping to be right is not be the wisest course to take in life, let alone in eternity. Share with him that the same God who allows him to do and believe what he likes is also his Creator, who loves him and has provided a wonderful future for him; he need only believe.

For the time is come that judgment must begin at the house of God: and if it first begin at us, what shall the end be of them that obey not the gospel of God? And if the righteous scarcely be saved, where shall the ungodly and the sinner appear? (1 Pet 4:17-18)

CHAPTER 6

HOW TO GET IT

Believe

*For the message of the cross is foolishness to those who are perishing,
but to us who are being saved it is the power of God.*

(1 Cor 1:18, NKJV)

To gain salvation from sin and its consequences, one must believe the Gospel of Christ. Perhaps the most common objection to faith, the "how" of salvation, is that simply believing is not sufficient, a topic covered in Chapter 4. Other objections to simple faith in the Gospel message include denying the need for belief, replacing belief with religious activities, and equating the Gospel with the faith claims of other religions. Some dismiss faith, claiming that truth cannot be known, while others define faith incorrectly, considering it an unproven "leap in the dark." But contrary to the idea of a blind leap of faith, God provided a large book of evidence for the Christian faith to rest upon. Whether by denying the simplicity, exclusivity, or necessity of it, those who deny that believing is the way to access salvation do have faith in something, even if it only in their own surmising. Reasoned explanations to their objections may help hearers to place their faith in Jesus Christ and His payment for the sins of the world.

Therefore it is of faith, that it might be by grace... (Romans 4:16a)

"Jesus died for the sins of the world, so everyone is saved. They may not know Jesus, but He still died for their sins."
"All roads lead to heaven."

He that believeth on him is not condemned: but he that believeth not is condemned already, because he hath not believed in the name of the only begotten Son of God. (Jn 3:18)

Denying that faith is the condition for salvation can take a "Christian" or non-Christian form. Some "believe in Jesus" in such a way as to conclude that everyone has already been saved because of Him. The non-Christian version of this is the idea of universal salvation regardless of one's brand of religion. Christianity is accused of narrow-mindedness for requiring a condition, or for claiming the one and only way of salvation, but it is the idea of universal salvation which is narrow, offering only one destiny to all, while God offers two. The Gospel provides a choice: to heaven or hell, to communion or separateness, to believe or reject the will of our Creator.

Denying the requirement of faith is a larger objection than simply denying the existence of a condition for salvation. It denies the word of God which declares it, the Christian's calling to proclaim it, and the choice of man to refuse or accept it. This objector may think himself generous and compassionate for releasing others from the requirement to believe the Gospel, but he is actually making himself a barrier to salvation. Denying that a condition exists may seem to him to eliminate the threat of hell, but offering false hope does the opposite of what he intends. To be saved from the penalty of sin, each person must believe the Gospel of Christ, found in 1 Corinthians 15:1-4.

"What about the people who haven't heard?" (aka "What about the guy in Bongo Bongo?")

For this is good and acceptable in the sight of God our Saviour; Who will have all men to be saved, and to come unto the knowledge of the truth. (1 Tim 2:3-4)

The objection that we affectionately call "the guy in Bongo Bongo" is based on an imaginary man who has never heard the Gospel. The assumption made is that there are people who have no awareness of Christianity, which therefore implies the need for an alternate way to be saved. How we are saved is by hearing the Gospel, but since this is supposedly not available, God must accept whatever religious effort is made by "the guy in Bongo Bongo."

Despite the fact that man does as he wishes in rebellion against God, he remains persistently religious. When the human spirit is not used in accordance with its function to commune with God, man seeks another means of fulfillment, practicing religious rituals to elicit a response from his "god." One could conclude that the existence of false religion means that remote peoples are not able to find the truth.

Perhaps because of the influence of The Theory of Evolution, the perception exists that remote peoples are ignorant, involuntarily isolated, and have been doing very little for a very long time. Contrary to the notion that "primitive" peoples haven't "evolved," in actuality, remote societies have managed to survive, keeping themselves warm, fed, and sheltered. They have populated far-flung islands, made discoveries, and passed along survival skills for generations. They seem quite capable. Considering also that missionaries have been traveling and sharing information for two thousand years, we cannot assume that remote peoples have not heard.

From the Bible record we know that man has been man all along, with intelligence, skills, and abilities given by God. The "Bongo Bongo objection" is ultimately an attack on God's character, accusing Him of leaving people with no way to be saved. God, however, desires for all to be saved, because God is love. The existence of false religion does not mean that God has left some people with no way to find the truth, nor does it necessitate that God contradict His word and allow alternative ways of salvation. Bibles, churches, missionaries and believers are everywhere. This objector can be assured that God will get the truth of how to be saved to those who want to know Him.

If any man will do his will, he shall know of the doctrine...
(Jn 7:17a)

And ye shall seek me, and find me, when ye shall search for me with all your heart. (Jer 29:13)

Because that which may be known of God is manifest in them; for God hath shewed it unto them. For the invisible things of him from the creation of the world are clearly seen, being understood by the things that are made, even his eternal power and Godhead; so that they are without excuse... (Ro 1:19-20)

120

"Faith in the Christian gospel cannot be the only way to heaven. What about all the other religions?"

Jesus saith unto him, I am the way, the truth, and the life: no man cometh unto the Father, but by me. (Jn 14:6)

Some objections to faith in the Gospel take issue with its exclusivity. With a custom-designed way of salvation for everyone, this "politically correct" view of religion is defeated by the fact that every religious belief cannot be true. Some are clearly invented to control and manipulate its followers. Some are preposterous. They deny and contradict each other, and have completely different gods, scriptures, and ways of salvation. This objector may not have considered the fact that most other religious systems have exclusive claims as well. Denying Christianity because of its exclusivity eliminates every religion with an exclusive claim, a fact which neutralizes this objection.

There is another problem with reasoning that there may be a way of salvation while denying that Christianity is not that way. If Jesus is not the way of salvation, and a religion other than Christianity was "the one true faith," how would anyone know it? It would be an insurmountable problem to objectively evaluate all of the world's belief systems, evenly scoring each by its merits, historical accuracy, evidence, logic, and reasonableness in order to know what to believe. Many religions have been lost to history. What if one of those was "the one"? Thankfully we do not need to scour the earth to find the right one, nor settle for the conundrum of competing claims. The true God settled the question by revealing Himself to us. He stepped into time and changed the world forever. He provided a book that cannot be disproven and He changed the heart of man. Christianity is a "religion" like no other, not only because of the miraculous death, burial and resurrection of Jesus, but also because it stands alone in declaring that man cannot save himself. False religions can't guarantee anything; they can't prove anything, and they can't save. Our God, just as a loving father would, took it upon Himself to save us.

> *He saw that* there was *no man, And wondered that* there was *no intercessor; Therefore His own arm brought salvation for Him; And His own righteousness, it sustained Him.* (Isaiah 59:16 NKJV)

"So you're saying no Hindus or Muslims or Buddhists are saved?"
"So you're saying my grandma is in hell?"
"So your belief is right and everybody else is wrong?!"

No man can come to me, except the Father which hath sent me draw him: and I will raise him up at the last day. (Jn 6:44)

Sometimes an apparent objection to Christian faith is due to the realization that the Gospel of Christ precludes another way of salvation. The objector may be reacting out of concern for loved ones who believed something other than the Gospel. An objection of this sort can also be an attack on you as the messenger of the Gospel, as if you are a know-it-all, pronouncing the eternal destiny of others. The issue, however, is not about the beliefs of the Christian witness or anyone else; it is about what God has said in His word about how one is saved.

If someone has passed on, and what they believed is unknown, the hearer may take comfort in the character of the One who created us and died to save us. If the loved one wanted to know how to be saved, God would not keep the truth hidden. Here in America especially, it is unlikely that someone would get through life without ever hearing the Gospel, attending church or having access to a Bible. If an objector is accusing the witness of being a judge, this can be turned by pointing the hearer to scripture. The witness is not the authority, the Bible is. God's word explains salvation; the Christian witness is just a messenger.

When we share the message of salvation by faith alone, it can elicit strong emotion. Hearers may be aware of a very different system practiced by their loved ones. We can only be sensitive to their concern, and try to point them to the love and justice of God, as well as to how one is saved, by faith in the Gospel of Christ, found in 1 Corinthians 15:1-4.

"I believe in me." "I have my own beliefs." "You have your way; I have mine." "Let's agree to disagree." "All religions are equal; let's co-exist."

The next day John seeth Jesus coming unto him, and saith, Behold the Lamb of God, which taketh away the sin of the world. (Jn 1:29)

It can be challenging to witness to those who seem to be okay with everything. They aren't offended by the Gospel of Christ. They aren't threatened by it, and they don't seem concerned. They may have "faith" in everything or in nothing. They deny faith in Christ, not out of hostility, but out of apathy. They just want everyone to get along.

As Christians, we are not refusing to "co-exist" by testifying to the truth. We desire that others be saved so they may know the joy, love, peace and hope that salvation provides.

The "okay-with-everything" person may listen, therefore providing an opportunity for a witness to try to cultivate in him some concern for his future. This may be done by asking him if he thinks he has ever done anything wrong, and if he thinks that there may be accountability in the end for having done so. Someday we will all face death. If an afterlife exists, how does this objector plan to find its location and get there? If he believes in life after death, and in the meaningfulness of our life here, he may recognize that he has a few spots on his record, and that knowing how to access salvation is more important than he realized.

If this objector knows something of other philosophies and ideas of religion, he can be reminded that none have a solution to the problem of sin. If he does not know the differences among religions, a few basic facts about the major ones can be shared to demonstrate the impossibility of all their contradictory claims being true. It is not necessary to be an expert on world religion. Who God is, for example, can be presented as a simple comparison. The God of the Bible is a tri-unity; three persons exist in one spirit. Allah, the god of Islam, is a single god, alone in eternity. Buddhism has no personal god, while Hinduism claims that "all is god," expressed in millions of deities. Just that small amount of information makes the point that God cannot simultaneously be all these things. From there, the conversation can move to whether these "gods" provide evidence regarding the claims of their respective religious systems. If there is a creator and an afterlife, being right about how to gain salvation is of everlasting significance.

Tolerance, acceptance, and belief in oneself are admirable principles, and are useful for some things, but it is not wise to go your own way when you don't know where you are going.

"I don't need to understand the Bible; I take it by faith." "Faith is a blind leap, a leap in the dark." "I hope I make it."

Even as Abraham believed God, and it was accounted to him for righteousness. (Gal 3:6)

Some objections to faith as the way of salvation are not actually to faith, per se, but are due to a faulty definition of faith. A hearer may claim to have faith, but when asked about it, he describes it as a wish, not as a surety. A person with this view does not correctly understand faith, which must be directed at an object. In other words, faith is placed in something, such as a promise made by God. Faith in the Gospel of Christ is a conviction of mind regarding how one is saved, with Jesus Christ and His victory over sin as the object of faith.

The Bible defines faith as being "fully persuaded" that the facts being presented are true:

And being fully persuaded that, what He had promised, He was also able to perform. (Ro 4:21)

These all died in faith, not having received the promises, but having seen them afar off, and were persuaded of them, and embraced them, and confessed that they were strangers and pilgrims on the earth. (Heb 11:13)

Knowing therefore the terror of the Lord, we persuade men; but we are made manifest unto God; and I trust also are made manifest in your consciences. (2 Cor 5:11)

The Bible also teaches us that faith has substance and evidence:

Now faith is the substance of things hoped for, the evidence of things not seen. (Heb 11:1)

Each of us is to believe the good news of salvation because it is reasonable and true:

And he reasoned in the synagogue every Sabbath, and persuaded the Jew and the Greeks. (Acts 18:4; see also Acts 19:8, 28:23)

And that we may be delivered from unreasonable and wicked men: for all men have not faith. (2 Thess 3:2)

Unfortunately, some 19th century German philosophy seeped into Christian theology, promoting the idea that faith is a "leap." This idea is a perversion of Biblical faith and is, in fact, the opposite of faith. God's word is inerrant, and the truth of the Bible is evident. The salvation message is not, "Maybe you'll get to heaven, so cross your fingers." It is presented as a surety, and each hearer must come to a conviction as to whether it really is how one is saved.

"I don't know."
"Nobody can know."

These things have I written unto you that believe on the name of the Son of God; that ye may know that ye have eternal life, and that ye may believe on the name of the Son of God. (1 Jn 5:13)

This objection to faith for salvation is either an admission that an individual does not know what is true, or a denial that anybody can know what is true. Those who describe themselves as agnostic typically mean that they personally do not know what is true about God or salvation. Others take this further, ironically refuting the absolute claims of the Bible by making another absolute claim: that truth cannot be known by anyone. "How do you personally know that nobody else can know?" is a powerful question to ask a person who holds the latter view. It can be reasoned that if we cannot know that something is true, then neither can we know it is not true. Therefore, it could be true. If the hearer will accept this logic, he may be willing to consider the declaration in Romans 1 that God has revealed Himself to man, and therefore His revelation about how to be saved can be known.

"I already believe in God; I don't need all those details."
"You're being picky. Just believe in Jesus."

For if he that cometh preacheth another Jesus, whom we have not preached, or if ye receive another spirit, which ye have not received, or another gospel, which ye have not accepted, ye might well bear with him. (2 Cor 11:4)

Sometimes an objection to faith in the Gospel is characterized by an apparent aversion to defining terminology. Because salvation is by faith, one's faith must be placed in the correct object. Faith in the Gospel is not a general, nebulous belief, such as a belief in some "higher power" with no particular traits; therefore one cannot believe the Gospel of Christ without knowing its elements.

Christians who stand up for an accurate Gospel are sometimes accused of being picky or "legalistic," as though a clear and thorough Gospel presentation is the equivalent of adding law-works for salvation, an issue covered in Chapter 4. While there are those who promote legalistic requirements for salvation, the Gospel itself is a message, and a message is either transmitted accurately or inaccurately. To deny this is to put oneself in the odd position of defending inaccuracy. We, as authors, believe it is not "picky" to handle God's word carefully and share the Gospel accurately. The many objections within this book show that the Gospel can be misunderstood in a startling number of ways. The hearer who objects that it is good enough to "just believe in Jesus" needs to be pointed back to the Bible as the authority, and its explanation of who Jesus is, what he did, and why. To emphasize the point, he can be asked, for example, "If you only need to believe in Jesus, then my question is, Jesus who?" The reason for asking this is because every counterfeit Christian group has a fake Jesus, such as the Mormon "Jesus" who is a brother to Lucifer, and the Jesus of Jehovah's Witnesses, who is a created being. Other examples of fakes include the Jesus of the Koran, who sneaked off the cross, and the Jesus of present day Judaism, who was sneaked out of his grave. Saving faith is in the Jesus of the Bible, not a generic "Jesus" who cannot save. The

Bible states that there is another Jesus and another gospel, which is a warning not to be taken lightly. Genuine faith in the Gospel of Christ is believing the particulars of its saving message. No Christian witness should be ashamed of providing a detailed and accurate explanation of the Gospel.

"I was born a _____, and I'll die a _____." "There are so many denominations; how do I know yours is right?"

There is neither Jew nor Greek, there is neither bond nor free, there is neither male nor female: for ye are all one in Christ Jesus. (Gal 3:28)

Sometimes a person may object to faith in the Gospel of Christ because he believes that the one witnessing is trying to get him to change his denominational affiliation or to sever him from his beloved family church. But salvation is by faith, not by any particular church group, and any Christian denomination or assembly can contain both believers and unbelievers. The Gospel should be shared with any person who does not seem to understand it, or who is willing to hear, regardless of where he attends church, or whether he does at all.

To remove denominational differences as the issue in a witnessing situation, the hearer can be shown that the testimony of the Bible is what matters, not the particulars of a denomination. But what if the denomination is a problem? The elements of Gospel itself may suggest to the hearer that his church or denomination has issues. If so, emphasize that the Bible is the authority, and suggest that his pastor is best suited to explain why his teachings contradict historic Christianity and the Bible record, if indeed they do.

This objection could turn into a debate about denominations themselves, but God does not recognize denominations; He recognizes His children, those who believe the Gospel of Christ (1 Cor 15:1-4). In 1 Corinthians 1:10-13, Paul admonishes the church for dividing and following individuals and emphasizes that the Gospel is what matters. Many denominations believe the same fundamentals of the faith. They may have small differences or large ones, but for the purpose of this book, the issue of denominations is whether the differences between them affect one's salvation.

"I'm a Christian, but I don't believe in that 'born-again' stuff."

Being born again, not of corruptible seed, but of incorruptible, by the word of God, which liveth and abideth for ever. (1 Pet 1:23)

This objection to how one is saved may be either be a misunderstanding of terminology, or a denial of what the term "born again" represents. Faith in the Gospel results in a spiritual birth, also known as being born again. Many church attendees are unfamiliar with the idea of being born again and may simply need an explanation. Reviewing the who, what, why and how of the Gospel message may reveal that this person needs salvation or that he has already accepted the Gospel by faith, but has not been taught the terminology of his spiritual birth. More information about the spiritual birth can be found in Chapter 1.

Jesus answered and said unto him, Verily, verily, I say unto thee,
Except a man be born again, he cannot see the kingdom of God...
Marvel not that I said unto thee, Ye must be born again. (Jn 3:3, 7)

Blessed be the God and Father of our Lord Jesus Christ, who
according to His great mercy has caused us to be born again to
a living hope through the resurrection of Jesus Christ from the
dead... (1 Pet 1:3 NASB)

"You have to repent."
"You need to turn from sin."
"That's easy believism."

Of his own will begat he us with the word of truth... (Jas 1:18a)
Whosoever believeth that Jesus is the Christ is born of God...
(1 Jn 5:1a)

Some objections to the teaching of faith alone for salvation amount to a difference in the use of words and their definitions, such as in the disagreements among some Christians regarding the word "repent." We, as writers, believe that the concept of repentance is embedded within the meaning of saving faith; it is a change of mind from what was believed before, to agreement with the Gospel message. Some believe, however, that repentance is a change of behavior, describing it as "turning from sin." This definition implies a moral reform, which is contrary to gracious salvation.

The main problem with adding a promise of future behavioral improvement to the Gospel is that grace excludes works, and, therefore, the Gospel of Christ cannot include a performance standard. Additionally, no human being can promise what his future behavior will be. He may have good intentions, but that is no guarantee and therefore cannot be part of salvation, as it would make our status with God unknown and unknowable. Furthermore, the idea that one must "turn from sin" to be saved is impossible. If any person must enumerate his sins and then turn from them to get saved, he would never get saved nor would anyone. An unsaved person is spiritually dead; he cannot turn from sin nor obey the command to live according to God's will. Even if "turning from sin" is defined only as a mental determination to obey God, it still adds a requirement that is not in the Gospel of Christ. Although a general awareness of being separated from God because of sin is implied by the fact that we need a Savior, God does not require us to make any promises of future behavior in order to be saved.

Salvation is not "cleaning up your act," "turning over a new leaf," or "determining to forsake sin." Salvation is a spiritual birth resulting from believing the contents of a message, the Gospel of Christ. Recognizing sin and allowing the Holy Spirit to empower a God-honoring Christian life is part of maturity after one is saved.

If this objection is not about the particulars of repentance, it may be about salvation being by grace and nothing else, covered in Chapter 4. Listening and learning what a person means by repentance allows a Christian witness to correctly address the "how" of salvation and explain Biblical repentance. Convinced that there is something more to salvation than just believing a message, an objector may call salvation by faith alone "easy believism." Some hearers cannot believe that the Gospel is so simple and pure. But it has to be pure; it cannot be tainted with the works of a sinner. The phrase "by which also ye are saved," found in Paul's Gospel presentation makes it clear that its elements are sufficient to save.

"If you think you can just believe on your own, that's decisional regeneration—you think you saved yourself with your decision."
"We are too depraved by sin to believe."
"I was chosen."

So then faith cometh by hearing, and hearing by the word of God. (Ro 10:17)

If you hear this objection to faith for salvation, you may be speaking with a religiously sophisticated person. It could come from an unsaved person, or from a Christian who believes in a particular brand of theology. Your aim as a Christian witness is to ascertain whether this person's faith is in being chosen, or if it is in the work of Jesus on the cross.

Some believe that man is incapable of responding to the Gospel because being a sinner, he cannot exercise saving faith. Because the Bible calls us to hear and believe, our view as writers is that there is a difference between "deciding" and "believing." We do not agree that the call to believe is the equivalent of saving oneself through a decision. By defining faith as the Bible does, as being persuaded of facts, we are not deciding to believe, but have been convinced by God's word and the Holy Spirit that the Gospel of Christ is true.

For what saith the scripture? Abraham believed God, and it
was counted unto him for righteousness. ...He staggered not at
the promise of God through unbelief; but was strong in faith,
giving glory to God; And being fully persuaded that, what he
had promised, he was able also to perform. And therefore it was
imputed to him for righteousness. (Ro 4:3, 20-22)

Another variation of this objection is the contention that the condition that one must believe amounts to "doing something" to get saved. This view considers faith itself to be a work. When we believe, however, we are not "doing" anything, because the Bible specifically excludes faith as a work. It, in fact, contrasts faith and work as opposites:

But to him that worketh not, but believeth on him that justifieth
the ungodly, his faith is counted for righteousness. (Ro 4:5)

Faith in the Gospel of Christ is not a work done by me, but the recognition that somebody else did something for me, namely that Jesus died on the cross to pay for my sins (1 Cor 15:1-4).

"Yes I'm saved...as long as...." (I don't turn my back on Jesus ...I don't sin too much ...I don't commit the unpardonable sin ...I don't fall away ...I keep believing ...I repent when I sin)

Now unto him that is able to keep you from falling, and to present
you faultless before the presence of his glory with exceeding joy...
(Jude 1:24)

A "what-if" type of objection to faith is an outcome-based belief for which faith is not the determining factor of salvation. Salvation is secure only "if" one avoids some sins, limits others, or quickly repents afterward. Rejecting faith alone for salvation is ultimately a form of legalism, covered in Chapter 4; in this view, one's status as a Christian is not dependent upon the satisfactory sacrifice of Jesus, but upon oneself. Committing a particular sin may cancel the payment He made on the cross.

Another version of this objection to the "how" of salvation is something we call "fruit inspection," meaning that salvation is determined by whether or not a person is bearing fruit. If he is not, he has lost his salvation or was never saved at all. The problem with this notion quickly becomes apparent when the objector is asked to define fruit, to quantify the amount and frequency of fruit needed to prove salvation, and by what calculation it will be measured.

These "what-if" objections make the Christian life into a maintenance plan to stay saved, as if the sacrifice of Christ was not sufficient to do so. One must keep bearing fruit or be careful to avoid certain sins in order to stay saved. There is no security in such a system; if our sins are not fully paid, we aren't actually saved from anything. According to this objection, Christians continue to be at risk of hell, making the entire concept of "being saved" meaningless.

The source of this objection is sometimes due to confusion between God's parental discipline of the believer and the final judgment of the unsaved. Bible verses which relate to the Christian's loss of rewards are misunderstood to mean a loss of one's saved status. The Bible, however, teaches that believers are "sealed unto the day of redemption" by the Holy Spirit, Himself, and we are, therefore, secure. The question for this objector is, "If you did turn your back on Jesus, isn't that just another sin He paid for?"

Now he which stablisheth us with you in Christ, and hath anointed us, is God; Who hath also sealed us, and given the earnest of the Spirit in our hearts. (2 Cor 1:21-22)

In whom ye also trusted, after that ye heard the word of truth, the gospel of your salvation: in whom also after that ye believed, ye were sealed with that holy Spirit of promise... (Eph 1:13)

And grieve not the holy Spirit of God, whereby ye are sealed unto the day of redemption. (Eph 4:30)

The Bible verse which does command us to do "fruit inspection" is in regard to the teaching of false prophets:

Beware of false prophets, which come to you in sheep's clothing, but inwardly they are ravening wolves. Ye shall know them by their fruits. (Mt 7:15-16a; see also 2 Pet 2:1)

Believers are to walk in holiness, bear fruit, and repent if they fall into sin. Doing such things, however, does not determine salvation. They are a result of salvation, and a product of spirituality as a Christian learns and grows in the faith. How we are saved is by grace through faith. The grace that saves us, keeps us, or what Jesus provided on the cross cannot be considered salvation.

"Yes I'm saved. I...." (...prayed the sinner's prayer ...was baptized ...was confirmed ...went forward at an altar call ...asked Jesus into my heart ...gave my life to Jesus ...made a decision for Christ ...made Jesus the Lord of my life)

Forasmuch as ye know that ye were not redeemed with corruptible things, as silver and gold, from your vain conversation received by tradition from your fathers; But with the precious blood of Christ, as of a lamb without blemish and without spot: Who verily was foreordained before the foundation of the world, but was manifest in these last times for you, Who by him do believe in God, that raised him up from the dead, and gave him glory; that your faith and hope might be in God. (1 Pet 1:18-21)

Some responses to discussions of faith are not so much objections as they are a failure to distinguish between faith and a church activity or ceremony which accompanied faith. This is sometimes due to well-intentioned people who have developed creative ways to explain or provide "easier access" to the Gospel...other than just explaining the Gospel. An example of this is the ubiquitous "Ask Jesus into your heart." Making such a statement may or may not accompany an understanding of the Gospel. Doing so, however, is not the equivalent of believing the content of the Gospel of Christ, and could therefore give false hope to someone who made the request but does not understand the who, what, why and how of the Gospel.

Similarly, the use of popular Christian phrases, such as "following Jesus" or "turning your life over to Jesus" are sometimes assumed to be understood by hearers to mean salvation by grace through faith in the elements contained in the Gospel of Christ. Short-cut phrases without definitions are certainly not intended to obscure the Gospel, but they can and do.

When speaking with someone who gives a testimony which adds a condition to faith in the Gospel of Christ, ask him to explain his conversion experience and learn as much as possible about what he thinks saved him. Does he, for example, think that the prayer he prayed saved him? Does he think he would be saved had he not been baptized with water? Rather than debating the efficacy of baptism or some other tradition, bring the discussion back to the content of the Gospel and its call to simply believe.

Going through the elements of the Gospel may reveal if this objector's faith is misplaced, as well as help him to see that the activity or ritual in question is not included in its message. Sinners are not offering Almighty God anything; we are asked to accept what *He* did. In faith, we look away from our own perceived goodness and self-righteousness, and recognize the work of another. No works done, no goodness maintained, no sin repented of or prayer sincerely prayed can save us. Only Jesus saves, and He saves through the Gospel message, by faith, stated as clearly as it could be in 1 Corinthians 15:1-4.

CHAPTER 7

WHERE TO FIND IT

The Bible

...it is written...

At least eighty verses in the Bible include the phrase, "it is written." God continually directs us to His written word. An objection about the Bible is an objection to the Gospel's source of authority. Without the record of the Bible, we have no authoritative source of information about God. God chose the written word to create a record of His communication with mankind. In comparing this written record with his miraculous experiences, Peter calls the scripture "a more sure word of prophecy," preserving God's message throughout time (2 Pet 1:19). John warns that those who "believeth not the record that God gave of his Son" are calling God a liar (1 Jn 5:10b).

Trusting the Bible matters, since it is where we find the message of salvation. Sometimes objections to the scriptures are merely bait for an argument or parroted criticisms; having no convictions of his own, the objector who denies the Bible's reliability may be willing to hear the Gospel if his objections are answered. However, if he rejects the Bible as God's word, offering verses or asking him to place his faith in its message may be premature, even hardening his resolve to stand against it. We do not recommend pressing a person who is not open. A willingness to consider the evidence of the Bible's trustworthiness, and a recognition of it as a reliable source of information is an important foundation for believing the Gospel of Christ, found in 1 Corinthians 15:1-4.

"The Bible is full of errors and contradictions."
"It couldn't possibly be the same Bible after 2000 years."
"It has been changed by the translators."
"There is no way that _____ happened."

But the word of the Lord endureth for ever. And this is the word which by the gospel is preached unto you. (1 Pet 1:25)

When an objector claims that the Bible has mistakes and translation problems, he should be asked to cite them. If he is unable to offer any contradictory verses or erroneous information, he may drop his objection and be willing to hear. However, if he is a studied objector and is able to voice examples for which you have no explanation, do not feel that you must have an immediate answer. You can thank him for the question, and tell him that you will do some research and get back to him. The question he raises can be an opportunity to show him that you are both willing to help him and able to uphold the authority of the Bible.

You performed signs and wonders in Egypt and have continued them to this day, in Israel and among all mankind, and have gained the renown that is still yours. (Jer 32:20 NIV)

"It's a good book, but it's not inspired."
"It was written by men."

All scripture is given by inspiration of God..." (2 Tim 3:16a)

Most Christians have probably heard the old canard that the Bible was written only by men. Some of the same people who believe that there is a psychic connection between thinking about a friend and then receiving a call from him, find it hard to believe that God could inspire a person to write. This objector may not realize that he is putting himself in the role of Bible expert with his denial of its divine origin. Since the Bible says that it is inspired by God, this objection is one of those occasions when a hearer simply has to decide for himself if he believes the record of scripture, or if he is interested enough to learn more about the evidence of its supernatural character. A Christian witness can ask the hearer if he would like to see what the Bible says about itself, offering verses which show that the doctrine of the inspiration of scripture is not a matter of opinion, but a foundation of Christianity:

> *For the prophecy came not in old time by the will of man: but holy men of God spake as they were moved by the Holy Ghost.*
> (2 Pet 1:21)

"That's your opinion; this is what it means to me."
"You can make the Bible mean anything you want."

Knowing this first, that no prophecy of the scripture is of any private interpretation. (2 Pet 1:20)

Upon being presented with the Gospel, a hearer may reveal that he considers the Bible a nice inspirational book, but that its contents are only a matter of opinion. If he has had some exposure to the Bible, he may have some favorite passages to which he has assigned his own interpretation and personal meaning, but does not consider them to have any broader significance. His underlying objection to the Gospel could be one of many, and will hopefully be uncovered with further discussion.

In addressing the objection to Bible meaning, the point needs to be made that every word has a definition, and cannot mean "anything you want." If it were not so, people would not be able to communicate with each other at all. For example, if he opened a cookbook and looked at a recipe, could he make it mean anything? The answer is obvious.

You may receive a follow-up objection which is that many words have multiple meanings. This is true, but even so, a word's meaning is narrowed by both its immediate and, in the case of the Bible, its historical context. If asked, the hearer who makes this claim will not be able to produce a Bible passage that can mean anything. Using the Gospel passage as an example, you can show him that there is little room for variation in its interpretation.

In some cases this objection is related to the differences among various Christian denominations. As Christian witnesses ourselves, we have encountered hearers who are distressed by the existence of so many kinds of churches and the differences between them. We know, of course, that the fact that Christians disagree on the finer points of the faith is a far cry from being able to make the Bible mean anything. We can provide assurance that although we all have much to learn, the death, burial and resurrection of Jesus Christ for sins is what saves us, and on that point, Christians agree.

"I Just Don't Believe It."

In whom the god of this world hath blinded the minds of them which believe not, lest the light of the glorious gospel of Christ, who is the image of God, should shine unto them. (2 Cor 4:4)

Some with whom you speak will just say, "No." A person who will not assent to even the historical facts of the Gospel is probably not open to believing it. Others are not interested or do not care enough to even formulate an objection. This may be because they have not thought about it, or because they are not ready to get into the discussion. Offer what you can. If someone is not willing to hear, respect his feelings about it, perhaps asking him to talk again sometime in the future. Pursuing a discussion with someone who does not want to hear is not helpful for your relationship with him, for your testimony, or for the likelihood that he may be open in the future. It can be disappointing, aggravating and even painful to be shut down when you want to share good news. Remember that the Lord, in His boundless longsuffering and mercy, wants this person to be saved even more than you do. In the meantime, God protects his freedom to disbelieve, even allowing him to be blinded from something that is so clearly true. If he becomes willing to trust the source of the Gospel and hear it, we can rest in the assurance that our God is good; those who seek Him will eventually be saved (2 Co 3:15-16).

CHAPTER 8

OBJECTIONS TO WITNESSING

Can two walk together, except they be agreed? (Amos 3:3)

Objections regarding the Gospel do not only come from the unsaved. Some Christians object to sharing the Gospel, defending their position by reasoning that their upright lifestyle is their testimony, or that evangelism is not their spiritual gift. Others who object believe that one's standing with God is only known by God, and therefore it is pointless to try to determine whether another person is saved. Some consider it an insult to be asked about their beliefs, and are not willing to ask that question of others, especially of those who attend church or claim to be Christian. Still others feel that faith is private, and that it is not our business to ask such personal questions, but on the contrary, it is God who has made it our business.

We believe it is both our calling and the outworking of the love of Christ to share the Gospel. Doing so is not just for a few, nor is living uprightly a substitute for it. Furthermore, if a person's faith is none of our business, or if it cannot be determined, or if we are making ourselves judges by asking about it, it would seem that the church is mistaken about one of its primary missions.

But watch thou in all things, endure afflictions, do the work of an evangelist, make full proof of thy ministry. (2 Tim 4:5)

"You can't judge another man's heart."
"It's between them and God."

The heart is deceitful above all things, and desperately wicked: who can know it? (Jer 17:9)

Some who object to witnessing may consider an inquiry into someone's beliefs to be judgmental, unknowable, or off-limits. Such a person may interpret Jeremiah 17:9 to mean that we cannot determine what someone believes. "Only God knows their heart," is how this objection may be phrased. Similarly to other verses about man's heart, this verse from Jeremiah is related to making choices, and in this case is referring to whether to trust man or the Lord. Not knowing our own heart means we may not know what we would choose in any given situation, but the Lord knows all, and He calls mankind to trust Him. This verse does not preclude inquiring about what someone believes or understands.

This objection can become stronger if the one to whom you wish to witness is a church attendee. Unfortunately, asking a church-affiliated person about his beliefs sometimes elicits a response akin to accusing him of robbing the till. But failing to ascertain a member's beliefs can lead to problems for church formation, administration, and fellowship. Knowing who has access to the spirit of wisdom, and who remains dead in trespasses and sins, is important to the church body when selecting teachers and officers, for example (Eph 1:17, 2:1).

Evangelism is not about "judging hearts," but we certainly can and must make an effort to learn whether or not others understand and agree with the Gospel of Christ. If someone does not believe, the conversation is an opportunity for that person to hear and be saved. If he is a believer, the discovery is a blessing and an opportunity to enjoy fellowship in the truth.

There is Biblical evidence that those who are born again can be recognized. The church is called to fellowship with one another as partners in the Gospel:

Praying us with much intreaty that we would receive the gift, and take upon us *the fellowship of the ministering to the saints.*
(2 Cor 8:4)

Not forsaking the assembling of ourselves together, as the manner of some is; *but exhorting* one another: *and so much the more, as ye see the day approaching.* (Heb 10:25)

Christians are also warned not to enter into partnership with unbelievers:

Be ye not unequally yoked together with unbelievers: for what fellowship hath righteousness with unrighteousness? And what communion hath light with darkness? And what concord hath Christ with Belial? Or what part hath he that believeth with an infidel? And what agreement hath the temple of God with idols? For ye are the temple of the living God; as God hath said, I will dwell in them, and walk in them; and I will be their God, and they shall be my people. Wherefore come out from among them, and be ye separate, saith the Lord, and touch not the unclean thing; and I will receive you... (2 Cor 6:14-17)

Let no man deceive you with vain words: for because of these things cometh the wrath of God upon the children of disobedience.

*Be not ye therefore partakers with them. ...And have no fellowship
with the unfruitful works of darkness, but rather reprove them.*
(Eph 5:6-7, 11)

Since God calls the body of Christ to assemble and partner with the
saved and not to yoke or partake with the unsaved, we can conclude
that its members can determine who is who. Warnings about wolves
and false teachers tell us that unbelievers are within our assemblies,
and this should be a matter of concern (Acts 20:29, 2 Pet 2:1).

As Christian witnesses ourselves, if we have not heard someone's
testimony of the Gospel, or if we have heard ideas from him that seem
unusual for a believer to hold, we would rather assume that he may
need to hear the Gospel, than assume that because he attends church,
he does not need to hear it. He may believe it, but has never been asked
to explain it, and may therefore have difficulty doing so. A conversation
about the Gospel, even for the purpose of helping someone learn to
articulate it more clearly, is worthwhile. "Leaving it between them and
God" benefits no one.

If you are not convinced that some in your local assembly may benefit
from having a conversation about the Gospel, try asking three or four
acquaintances if they would be willing to explain it to you as they
would when they share it. You may be surprised by the variety of
presentations that you hear.

It is not judging a person or his heart by making an attempt to determine
if a person understands, believes, or is able to articulate the Gospel by
which we are saved. Settling for, "I'm a Christian," as a response to a
question about salvation could be an everlasting mistake.

"Evangelism is not my gift."

Some Christians believe that evangelism should only be done by those who are gifted to do so, and that the lack of the gift excuses them from sharing the Gospel. Contrary to the idea that the presence or absence of a spiritual gift releases us from responsibility for acts of Christian service, throughout scripture we find that the church is called to evangelism, hospitality, giving, encouraging, teaching, and serving one another. There is no exclusion based on gifting. For example, Paul says that it is good to desire to be a bishop, not limiting it to those gifted as pastors. All Christians are thoroughly furnished unto all good works, possessing power for all things pertaining to life and godliness:

*All scripture is given by inspiration of God, and is profitable for doctrine, for reproof, for correction, for instruction in righteousness: That the man of God may be perfect, **throughly furnished unto all good works**.* (2 Tim 3:16-17; emphasis added)

*Grace and peace be multiplied unto you through the knowledge of God, and of Jesus our Lord, According **as his divine power hath given unto us all things that** pertain **unto life and godliness,** through the knowledge of him that hath called us to glory and virtue...* (2 Pet 1:2-3; emphasis added)

*This is a true saying, **If a man desire the office of a bishop, he desireth a good work**.* (1 Tim 3:1; emphasis added)

*For, brethren, ye have been called unto liberty; only use not liberty for an occasion to the flesh, but **by love serve one another.*** (Gal 5:13; emphasis added)

*Let the word of Christ dwell in you richly in all wisdom; **teaching and admonishing one another** in psalms and hymns and spiritual songs, singing with grace in your hearts to the Lord.* (Col 3:16; emphasis added)

*That they may **teach the young women** to be sober, to love their husbands, to love their children.* (Titus 2:4; emphasis added)

*Wherefore **comfort yourselves together, and edify one another,** even as also ye do.* (1 Thess 5:11; emphasis added)

*But **exhort one another daily,** while it is called today; lest any of you be hardened through the deceitfulness of sin.* (Heb 3:13; emphasis added)

***Every man according as he purposeth in his heart,** so let **him give**; not grudgingly, or of necessity: for God loveth a cheerful giver.* (2 Cor 9:7; emphasis added)

The body of Christ needs support and care, and the world needs deliverance from sin. Accordingly, God empowers every believer to do His will, by the power of His grace. The scripture calls all believers to build up and to serve the body of Christ in a variety of ways, as well as to proclaim the good news of 1 Corinthians 15:1-4 to the world.

"I show by my conduct that I am Christian; If someone asks, I will share the gospel."

So then faith cometh by hearing, and hearing by the word of God.
(Ro 10:17)

1 Peter 3:15 is sometimes used to support what we will call "lifestyle evangelism." Rather than asking others if we may share the Gospel, in this view, Christians are to simply live an upright life of morality and service, waiting for someone to ask us why we live the way we do. Those who hold this view consider their life to be their "witness" to others. Here is the verse in context:

> *14 But and if ye suffer for righteousness' sake, happy are ye: and be not afraid of their terror, neither be troubled; 15 But sanctify the Lord God in your hearts: and be ready always to give an answer to every man that asketh you a reason of the hope that is in you with meekness and fear: 16 Having a good conscience; that, whereas they speak evil of you, as of evildoers, they may be ashamed that falsely accuse your good conversation in Christ.*
> (1 Pet 3:14-16)

Waiting to be asked about our faith could leave us waiting a very long time. Living in accordance with our faith gives credibility to our testimony, but does not replace it. A witness, such as in a courtroom, is called to verbally testify; he is not called to the stand to be silently observed. An unsaved person can live a decent, moral life, be a good citizen, do good deeds, and have a good attitude. How then would his lifestyle be distinguished from ours? The Christian would be no more likely to be asked than he would. Because faith comes by hearing, we must boldly testify (Ro 10:17).

The context of 1 Peter is not witnessing, but suffering. Suffering weakens its victims, so Peter exhorts Christians to remain holy in order to avoid slander and accusations, ready to give a reason for the hope we have beyond the suffering. He is describing a spiritual response when under a time of testing. Nothing in the passage exempts us from sharing the Gospel nor cancels our calling to evangelize.

If you hear a Christian brother object to witnessing, consider offering to work together with him in order to build his confidence to do it. Working together can be an opportunity to explore agreement and gain understanding in other areas of church teaching. We can build stronger churches, families and friendships if we discuss together the doctrines that we know well and search the scriptures together to gain an understanding of those we do not know. The more doctrine we understand, the more easily we can discuss it with hearers. Since we all have much to learn, we encourage each reader to have faith in God's promise that He provides us with both the desire and the ability to do His will. Your faith will be rewarded with opportunities to share the Gospel by which we are saved, found in 1 Corinthians 15:1-4.

For it is God which worketh in you both to will and to do of his good pleasure. (Phil 2:13)

For after that in the wisdom of God the world by wisdom knew not God, it pleased God by the foolishness of preaching to save them that believe. (1 Cor 1:21)

It Is God Who Saves

And the LORD passed by before him, and proclaimed, The LORD, The LORD God, merciful and gracious, longsuffering, and abundant in goodness and truth... (Ex 34:6)

Believing that we had heard it all, we challenged a friend to give us an objection that was not in this book. She did. In fact, she had just heard it. An ailing, elderly person to whom she had been witnessing told her that he did not want to accept the Gospel because he was afraid that if he did, he would die right then. She was confounded by his response, and we both admitted we had not heard it before. Upon consideration, we concluded that a person afraid of dying has doubts as to whether the afterlife is better than this life. At its core, his fear is a doubt about the character of God and whether He is true to His promises, a "who He is" objection.

God is good, has a good intention for all of us, and will wait long for our repentance. God loved us in Christ, by sending the Son to die for all the sins of the world. Hopefully this hearer will be open to learning more about God's goodness. The eternal consequences of forfeiting the gift of salvation is so horrible that the idea of allowing someone to slip away without hearing it drives our efforts to be witnesses.

A passion for sharing the Gospel is a wonderful thing to have, and it is best tempered with the knowledge that we are often only seed-planters, and always servants. It is God who saves. We do what we can, but if someone isn't ready, or says, "No," there is no value in pressing him or in being hard on oneself about it. For some, the Gospel is a lot to take in; eternity is a lot to think about. New information often forms questions in a hearer's mind as he thinks of things he had no occasion to consider before. We have spoken with people who genuinely do not know what they believe. After hearing the Gospel, they required time to think and to process what they heard before they had any response to it at all.

We can trust our good God to make every effort to save. Sometimes the process is a long one, and we as Christian witnesses never see the results. But we can rest in the knowledge that the Holy Spirit is doing His part, convincing the hearer of the truths presented. God wants our spouse, child, loved one, and friend to be saved much more than we do! If they are open to the Gospel, they will come to believe it.

The Gospel by which we are saved is clearly articulated in 1 Corinthians 15:3-4, within the context of verses 1-8. When we share it but do not receive the desired response, offering a "short-cut" to the hearer may be tempting, but we must never stray from God's saving message. Encouraging a "decision for Christ" or leading a prayer may seem harmless, but responses to such things can be made without understanding. An on-the-spot profession can short-circuit the process of allowing the hearer to thoughtfully consider the reasonableness of the Gospel, or interfere with the ministry of the Holy Spirit to truly convict the hearer of sin and convince him of the truth.

The Gospel of Christ is not a formula, or an incantation, or "magic words" that one can say to be saved. Neither is God's word a secondary source to confirm a sign or an experience. A person who imagines that he has become a believer because he has witnessed a miracle, for example, has only become a believer in the miracle. The Gospel of Christ, found in 1 Corinthians 15:1-4, is a particular message which we are to believe in order to receive the gift of salvation.

Every word of scripture is God-breathed. We must handle, speak, and share God's word with accuracy, as the holy gift from heaven that it is. We may need to educate our Christian friends about the importance of doing so. We may face persecution as we attempt to engage both Christians and non-Christians into conversations about the Gospel and other Bible topics, but we can stand against the "politically correct" social rules which intimidate Christians into silence. We can and should talk about what matters, whether of this world, or of the next. We need not bow to the Ruler of this Age whose singular purpose is to thwart the blessings of God to mankind. He will not ultimately succeed, but neither will we give him aid. Sometimes our efforts will succeed, sometimes not. We share the Gospel. It is God who saves.

"Ruthie"

At least annually for twenty years, a friend of ours heard the Gospel from one of us or from both. She was known for charitable giving within her community. She helped her neighbors and helped at church. She made contributions to college scholarships and made quilts for the homeless. She certainly would not have made a silly claim such as that her quilt-making, for example, was a ticket into heaven, and yet she believed in a general sense that doing good works is part of a person's qualification to get there.

Every time we visited Ruthie, she asked us questions about the Bible, and wanted to talk about salvation. Every time we explained it she had the same response: "I can't believe I don't have to do anything." It bothered her and she had no peace, so we had essentially the same conversation year after year:

"What about the verses on works? I can't believe I don't have to do anything."

"But that is what grace is. It literally means "undeserved favor" and God is exercising grace by saving us. If we had to do works to get salvation, it would not be a gift. It would not be undeserved; it would be earned. When you earn something, the one you work for is indebted to you. They owe you for the work you did. Do you think that you can in-debt God to you? Do you think you can stand before Him on judgment day and tell Him that you were good and so He owes you heaven?"

"Well, no, that seems presumptuous. But so does assuming that I can just get in for nothing."

"You aren't getting in for nothing. You were given a gift by someone who did the work for you. You are accepting what Jesus did on your behalf. He did the work, so to speak, and it wasn't nothing."

"But I believe that."

"Yes, but you don't believe that what He did is enough. You think that you have to do something."

"So what about all the things in the Bible that God says He wants us to do?"

"Well, He does want us to do good things. But those things are not a way to get into heaven. Good works are a result of salvation. The way into heaven is by believing the Gospel of Christ. Faith in what Jesus did on the cross for sin is the method God provided for our salvation."

"What about the people who do really bad things?"

"We all rebel against God, and God considers all rebellion 'really bad'. But those sins were all paid on the cross. There are not some sins that are excluded from 'the sins of the world'. It includes everything. If it is available to the whole world, then it can't be about how good or bad someone is. If it is about believing in Him, then it can't be about what you or I do. Even if I do lots of wonderful things, it doesn't erase or wipe out my sins. Once I've sinned against God, I can't make up for it. I can't travel back in time and undo it or fix it. So, I already deserve the penalty for sin, no matter how many good things I do. Jesus Christ didn't have any sins on His account, so He was a pure and perfect sacrifice for sin. He paid for those sins for us, and all He asks is that we trust in His payment. That is faith; it is being persuaded that the Gospel is true, that Jesus died on the cross for your sins, and was buried and rose again, just as the Bible foretold."

"So I don't have to do anything?"

"No."

"Just believe it?"

"Yes."

"Even Hitler could get in?"

"Yes."

"I can't believe I don't have to do anything."

"I know."

A few weeks before she passed away, at 95 years old, she made a rare telephone call to us. She said, "I haven't been able to stop thinking about you. Will you be coming to visit?" She knew her life was nearly over and eternity was on her mind. Having just seen her three weeks earlier, we quickly made arrangements for another seven-hundred-mile drive to her home, hoping for one last chance to testify. Always having been fascinated with prophecy, she was a longtime viewer of the Jack Van Impe television show. She admired him because he knew so much scripture by heart. When we arrived, she was eager to tell us that she had written to Van Impe with her question, the same question she asked us every time we visited. She was very proud to say that he had written back. When he confirmed what she had heard so many times, that she was saved by faith alone, she finally believed, telling us, "Now I know that Jesus did it all."

> So shall my word be that goeth forth out of my mouth: it shall not return unto me void, but it shall accomplish that which I please, and it shall prosper in the thing whereto I sent it. (Isa 55:11)

> The Lord is not slack concerning his promise, as some men count slackness; but is longsuffering to us-ward, not willing that any should perish, but that all should come to repentance. (2 Pet 3:9)

Appendix

Index of Objections

Objections to who He is

Objections to what He did

Objections to why I need it

Objections to how to get it

Objections to where to find it

Objections to witnessing

Index of Bible Verses

by which we are saved

by which we are saved

Notes

by which we are saved

CPSIA information can be obtained
at www.ICGtesting.com
Printed in the USA
FFOW01n0937110617
36626FF